Video Violence and Children

Video Violence and Children

Edited by
Geoffrey Barlow
and
Alison Hill

ST. MARTIN'S PRESS   New York

All rights reserved. For information, write:
St. Martin's Press, Inc., 175 Fifth Avenue, New York, NY 10010
Printed in Great Britain

First published in the United States of America in 1985

ISBN 0-312-84571-5

Library of Congress Cataloging-in-Publication Data

Video violence and children.

Bibliography: p.
Includes index.
1. Television and children.   2. Violence in
television.   I. Barlow, Geoffrey.   II. Hill, Alison.
HQ784.T4V528   1985   305.2'3   85-14596
ISBN 0-312-84571-5

Contents

Foreword

Anyone concerned for the welfare of children – especially parents, teachers, social workers, leaders of young people's organisations – would do well to read this book. It does not make pleasant reading, but it compels us to face the reality of a new menace which threatens us.

The case is overwhelmingly made that 'video nasties' are seen by a surprisingly large percentage of the young, and that the effect on many of them is alarmingly harmful. That in itself should be a cause for gratitude to those who have taken this matter up and pursued it with care and persistence. It should also be a call to vigilance on the part of all who have contact with children, and a summons to make this evil more widely understood and to seek all possible means of resisting it.

I see this book as a serious warning in view of the fact that (to quote from Chapter 7): 'The availability of the home video could become virtually universal in Britain, as the television has done over the past thirty years . . . The video containing combinations of violence and sex is a potential mental and moral health hazard of a kind we have not experienced before.'

April 1985   *Donald Coggan*

Preface

I have been privileged to be Chairman of the informal Group of Parliamentarians and Churchmen who came together in 1983 with the common wish to take action to protect children against injury from violent and obscene video-tapes, which appeared to be circulating widely.

Obviously, the first step was to promote a research project which would find out what videos children were seeing throughout the country. We raised our finance from amongst ourselves and a number of generous friends, but the work was, in the main, done by an immense amount of voluntary expert labour. Here I must pay a special tribute to Dr Clifford Hill, the Director of the project, whose inspiration and enthusiasm have now brought it to a successful fulfilment. The full Report of our sociological field research was published in March 1984 – the first nationwide research on this important subject ever to be published here – with an interim Report the previous November.

This book completes the work of our Group with an analysis of an important piece of research, together with expert commentary by leading academics, doctors and educationalists. It is an informed attempt to analyse the picture which our research has thrown up, and thus to understand what effect this violent and obscene material is having on the children who see it.

At this time, when crimes of violence and sexual offences are on the increase, Parliament is deeply concerned with these matters, and has already placed on the Statute Book the Video Recordings Act to classify all video-tapes, as a first step to protecting families against offensive tapes. I believe this book will help to deepen the understanding of all who wish to see our young people growing up in a decent atmosphere and, as such, it has my warm support.

April 1985   Lord Nugent of Guildford, PC

The Contributors and Other Members of the Working Party

The Right Rev and Right
Hon Lord Coggan, PC, MA, DD

Former Archbishop of Canterbury

The Right Hon Lord Nugent
of Guildford, PC

Deputy Speaker, House of Lords,
Chairman of the Enquiry

The Right Hon Lord Swinfen,
JP, ARICS

Chairman of the Academic Working
Party of the Enquiry

Professor Sir Martin Roth,
MD, FRCP, FRCPsych, ScD

Professor of Psychiatry, University
of Cambridge; former President of
the Royal College of Psychiatrists

Dr Graham Melville-Thomas,
MB, FRCPsych, DPM

Child Psychiatrist, Cardiff;
Member of the Academic Working
Party

Dr Clifford Hill, MA,
BD, PhD

Former Senior Lecturer in Sociology,
University of London; Consultant
Sociologist to the Home Office,
Police and Prison Services;
Director of the Enquiry

Dr Geoffrey K. Nelson, BSc,
MSc, PhD

Principal Lecturer in Sociology,
City of Birmingham Polytechnic;
Consultant Sociologist to the
Research Team of the Enquiry

Miss Alison Hill, BA

Psychologist; Research Co-ordinator
of the Enquiry; Joint Editor

Professor Andrew Sims,
MD, FRCPsych

Professor of Psychiatry, University
of Leeds; Chairman of the Research
Council of the Royal College of
Psychiatrists; Member of the
Academic Working Party

Professor Peter Gray, MB, ChB, FRCP, DCH	Professor of Child Health, University of Wales College of Medicine, Cardiff; Member of the Academic Working Party
Mrs Pat Wynnejones, BA, Cert of Ed	Lecturer and writer; formerly Headmistress of two primary schools; Senior Lecturer in English at the Froebel Institute (Roehampton Institute of Higher Education); Member of the Academic Working Party
Dr Howard Davis, BA, PhD	Media Sociologist, Edinburgh; Member of the Academic Working Party
Mr Peter Liddelow, JP	Deputy Headmaster, Comprehensive School, London; Member of the Academic Working Party
Dr Robert Holman, BA, PhD	Former Professor of Social Administration; Community Worker, Bath; Member of the Academic Working Party
Mr Geoffrey Barlow	Writer, journalist and broadcaster; Joint Editor

Acknowledgments

As Chairman I would like to express my sincere thanks and deep appreciation of the very hard work put in to the Working Party by the distinguished academics of whom it was formed. I know that in very busy lives, they all made the time to undertake all the necessary detailed research that has been entailed in producing this book. In particular a note should be made of the unstinting efforts of the Director of Research, Dr Clifford Hill.

This research would have been made a great deal more difficult without the co-operation of the bodies for whom the members worked. In particular I should like to express my thanks for the considerable help given by the Department of Child Health of the University of Wales College of Medicine, and by Steve Kay of the College's Department of Computing. Mention must also be made of St James' University Hospital, Leeds and of Jane Boyce of The Royal College of Psychiatrists. We also had considerable help from Sue Creighton and Dr Alan Gilmour, of the National Society for the Prevention of Cruelty to Children.

I must not forget to mention the help with fund-raising from Lady Ingleby and the financial assistance that was given to us by all our sponsors, too numerous to name individually. In the realms of finance, The Order of Christian Unity very kindly ran our bank account.

I know that I have been unable, through lack of space, to name all the Research Team and voluntary helpers who were with us for some or all of the time spent in undertaking the research and producing this book. However, I would like to thank Mrs Jean Wolton who typed the manuscript of this book. Mention must also be made of Renault UK Ltd, who provided a car for the research team for nearly a year. Finally, I wish to express my personal thanks to my own employers, John Grooms Association for the Disabled, who never once questioned the numerous, and often long periods of absence from my office when engaged in the work, over nearly two years, that has gone in to the preparation of this book.

April 1985   Lord Swinfen

1 Introduction: The Socio-Psychological Phenomenon of Violence

Martin Roth

The last decade has seen a significant change in attitudes towards the effects of transmitting scenes of extreme violence and brutality on the television screen. The transformation has been so radical in character that it is to be doubted whether this book would have found a publisher ten years ago. Yet the problem was already manifest in its essentials, although it has grown to disturbing proportions in the intervening years. It is difficult to be certain about the factors responsible for the change in opinion but some influences can be seen as having played a part.

Until the mid 1970s, most surveys conducted into the effects of viewing scenes of violence ended with conclusions, of a negative, or ambiguously poised character. The majority of the large studies in this field have been conducted in the United States and the two main landmarks – the commissions of enquiry which followed the assassination of John and Robert Kennedy and that which was initiated by President Johnson in 1967 – conformed to this pattern in the conclusions they reached.

The report of the first of these commissions called into question any direct influence by violence shown on television on the behaviour of children. The second appeared unable to draw any clear conclusions from a large body of evidence.

In his chapter, Dr Melville-Thomas has drawn attention to the strong disinclination of those reared in a liberal tradition to face squarely the possible need for closer scrutiny and greater control of what can be transmitted. There is considerable weight in this point and the tradition to which it refers extends back down the centuries to the Reformation. Any attempt to place controls upon freedom to communicate by whatever medium, conjures up the bigoted despots who interrogated Galileo and burned heretics at the stake or those other tyrants who prohibited music, the theatre and dancing in a fanatical pursuit of dogmas that had lost all contact with real human values and needs.

The repugnance for censorship is understandable. But, it overlooks the fact that it has existed ever since men first came together in societies. The problem is, and has always been, where to set the limits and this question has to be addressed anew with each major social and technological development. One factor which has probably acted as a catalyst in accelerating the change in outlook has been the appearance and rapid proliferation of video films which depict scenes of unprecedented violence, brutality and sadistic cruelty often with a sexual content. The direct transmission of such material on television would have contravened the law in this country.

The awakening of public concern witnessed in the past three years has stemmed in part from a statement by Mr Wardell, Member of Parliament for Gower, who appealed to the House of Commons in the autumn of 1982 (while introducing a Private Members Bill that was to prove abortive) to enact means for the protection of young children from the danger they might suffer through exposure to such materials.

A significant new development was the report *Television and Behaviour: Ten Years of Scientific Progress and Implications for the 1980s* published in 1982 in the USA. It drew quite different conclusions from the previous Presidential Commissions of Enquiry to which reference has already been made. As the US National Institute for Mental Health had sponsored the investigation, the conclusion reached by this enquiry that there was a direct causal connection between television violence and real life violence was given an added authority. And television violence is still qualitatively apart as well as different in degree from the noxious blend of cruelty, violence, black magic and sexual brutality which clearly emerges from the summaries of the video films recorded in Appendix 3 of this book.

When they embarked on their enquiries into the effects of video film violence on children, the sponsors, the all-party group of Members of Parliament and the widely representative body of distinguished men and women who constituted their working party, encountered a surprising volume of seemingly concerted opposition and hostility. A number of press reports from ostensibly disinterested sources gave inaccurate and tendentious accounts of the contents and character of the interim report. Some of these were traced back to sections of the video industry. Some analyses of the scientific qualities of the Report were found to have emanated from individuals connected with the industry. The experience was salutary and could perhaps, in retrospect, have been anticipated. For the Report provided preliminary evidence that large numbers of school children were viewing video films that could not have been legally exhibited in this country even in cinemas restricted to adults.

Both this book and the second part of the enquiry, the results of which are summarised by Dr Nelson in Chapter 4, are descriptive in character. But it is plain that the authenticity and reliability of the responses recorded in the questionnaires were submitted to scrupulous and detailed checks. Surveys of this nature are an indispensable first step for the stringent scientific investigation of psychological problems. Their value to this end and the attention that their practical implications should command, must always be contingent upon the extent to which the research workers have shown themselves able to lean over backwards to permit their hypotheses and preconceptions to be refuted by their own findings. In the opinion of the author of this chapter the Report satisfies this criterion of quality and reliability by an ample margin.

The results are of great social importance and deserve close attention from Parliament and all sections of the community. It is a matter of grave concern that in the formative years, from the ages of seven to seventeen years, 45% of children should have seen one or more video films which would legally be classed as obscene in this country on account of the morbid, sadistic and repugnant nature of the violence they portray. The first knowledge of sexual life acquired by these children may come from viewing films in which sexual conduct is inextricably entwined with violence, hatred, coercion and the humiliation of women in particular. As the summaries of selected films in Appendix 3 reveal, the violence emanates mainly from men but an increasingly conspicuous feature of the 'video nasties' has been the return of the violence with a vengeance, by the women. And in some cases they are the initiators of vicious and sexually brutal behaviour towards the opposite sex.

The attitudes of parents are paramount in deciding whether or not children are at risk of exposure and the children of 'lenient' parents witnessed 'video nasties' more often than those judged 'protective'. Many parents seemed in total ignorance of the new influence which was entering the lives of their children. As the report from the Educationalists in Chapter 9 points out, the connection between violent behaviour on the one hand and exposure to video films on the other, is difficult to establish in a conclusive manner. Tentative as it is, the evidence provided in this chapter, including the self-reports from children who had behaved viciously, has qualities of authenticity that create a compelling need for action.

There is at least prima facie evidence that the emotional health of some children is being undermined. Although the steep escalation in violence among children and young people in schools comes from a conglomeration of causes the effect of an entirely new kind of direct influence upon the mental lives of children which provides explicit models of inhumane and sadistic conduct cannot, and must not, be ignored. It would be prudent to assume that these models are being to some extent emulated and incorporated into their repertoire of behaviour patterns.

The evidence from 404 consultant and senior registrar child and adolescent psychiatrists points in the same direction. If these professional men and women had any preconceptions, their training would have inclined them to explain the aggressive and related propensities of children in terms of genetical or constitutional factors or of psychodynamic influences emanating

from failure to negotiate successfully one of the stages of emotional development defined by psychoanalysts. A proportion of psychiatrists would have
allowed for the operation and interaction of both groups of factors. In the
light of this, the fact that with a 75% response rate the psychiatrists should
have unanimously agreed that violent videos frequently made significant
contributions to the symptoms displayed by their patients the survey has to
be accorded considerable weight as evidence; the measure of concordance
with the observations of Paediatricians (described in Chapter 8) and Educationalists is impressive.

In assessing the views and the work undertaken by a group of scientists
and laymen, whose endeavours were motivated by common concerns and
common purposes, it is essential to maintain an objective and critical stance.
This is particularly the case when they have focused on one possible factor
within a complex network of causal agents. Careful consideration has to be
given to the possibility that they may have got the picture out of perspective
and out of proportion. It is all the more important to apply critical and
objective scrutiny to the findings and the claims when one of the consequences may be some restriction in freedom of communication and expression. As already pointed out, censorship has been upheld and execrated
down the centuries for very good reasons.

It may be objected, for example, that the effects exerted by video violence
are too trivial in relation to the far more powerful social and familial factors in
operation to justify legally enforceable prohibitions. However, the view that
video violence is negligible in its effects is refuted by the unanimous
testimony of representative groups of specialists whose work brings them
into daily contact with children and young people, both mentally ill,
disturbed or seemingly normal and intact in mental health. The implications
of the surveys described by Miss Alison Hill, and by Dr Geoffrey Nelson in
Chapters 4 and 5 are no less unequivocal. This evidence has to be viewed in
the context of new forms of violent conduct that are manifest both in schools
and elsewhere in society. The testimony from individual cases in which the
violence depicted on the videos has been exactly duplicated in the brutal acts
of children or the crimes committed by adults cannot, therefore, be dismissed as merely anecdotal.

At this point we have to confront the objection commonly voiced, that
such influences of video violence act with a specific and selective severity
upon those constitutionally pre-disposed. In other words, any aggression
that follows may be symptomatic of the emotionally immature and im-
balanced state of the individuals concerned, rather than a consequence of
exposure to video sadism. There is indeed evidence that hereditary factors
contribute to the genesis of violent and sexually brutal behaviour and to its
incorporation within the individual's patterns of conduct. But most of the
available testimony suggests that the environment in which the early formative years are spent makes a substantially greater contribution to variance in

respect of such conduct. It is not only the deprivation suffered, but the models set for possible emulation that are of fateful importance.

Another objection which enters is that the harmful effects attributed ignore the beneficial influences of catharsis which results from exposure to even extreme and deviant forms of violent and erotic behaviour. As a result of the identification with the person who enacts such conduct, the individual's aggressive drives may be reduced through being channelled along the safe patterns of fantasy. The balance of the evidence is strongly against significant benefit or mitigation from catharsis. Most of the testimony available at the present time, as Dr Melville-Thomas has pointed out, shows the effects of learning through modelling to predominate in the shaping of aggressive and violent behaviour. The lesson may be more easily learned by some personalities than others, although little is known of the contribution of such personality factors at the present time. It seems probable that the overwhelming majority of individuals are susceptible, to some extent, particularly in the impressionable period of childhood.

Admittedly, the video film is only one among a whole range of influences that determine the patterns of conduct the individual ultimately manifests in adult life. But when we turn to the most powerful of the sociofamilial influences upon the development of behaviour we find the proportion of one-parent families to have been rising for decades. It continues to escalate. The prevalence of marital disruption and divorce also continues to show a steep upward trend. As the proportion of women who expect to find employment outside the home expands the number of latch-key children mounts each year. The influence of the family continues to be important. For example, as the surveys reported in this book have shown the viewing of 'video nasties' by children correlates highly with the amount of viewing by their mothers.

But evidence from many sources indicates that the influence of family example and parental control have been waning in highly developed countries for some decades, while the effect of models set outside the family exert a proportionately greater influence. Similar statements can be made about education which also has a potentially far-reaching influence and should at its best, impart values as well as knowledge and vocational skills. These values should not merely mirror those that predominate in the immediate social and political scene, they should transcend them. But the power and impact of the school are being steadily eroded by that of the screen. Evidence from the USA and to a lesser extent, from this country, shows children to be spending as many or more hours in viewing as in the classroom.

In the view of some critics, social influences will be held to predominate in the shaping of human conduct and video violence and pornographic sadism will be classed among the less important of their multitudinous effects. Society will have to be radically transformed, it will be insisted, to bring about any modification of the conduct exemplified in violent videos or passively viewed on the screen. It is futile if not dangerous to force underground one unhealthy symptom of a deep-rooted social malady. Should coercive measures be adopted to suppress them, such symptoms will be likely to find expression in some other and possibly more malevolent form. But this attribution of power to shape without limit the behaviour of growing children to some transcendent metaphysical entity named 'society' should be viewed with scepticism. The human individual is more than a *tabula rasa* on which instructions and behavioural programmes from whatever source can be permanently engraved. Such views conflict with the evidence that derives from biology and leave little or no scope for human autonomy and integrity. Social influences exert their effects mainly through institutions such as the family and the school. And we return full circle to the evidence that testifies to the erosion of their authority in recent decades.

To equate the patterns of behaviour recorded in the types of video film that have prompted the enquiries in this book with the nursery rhymes and tales of witch-craft employed since time immemorial to distract children or to stir their imagination is to misconceive the situation entirely, as Professor Sims and Dr Melville-Thomas have pointed out. Brutalities are not enacted in the manner of playful pretence in some remote fairy land. They are carried out in familiar environments, in homes, bedrooms, railway trains and back streets. The identification of the viewer with the violent actor is fostered and reinforced. And there are some entirely new ingredients. The macabre and noxious brew of violent sexuality, superstition, and black magic, the infusion of the imagery of the Nazi era with its gas chambers and the permeation of sexual love with coercion often to the point of murder and dismemberment are novel features. They belong to a different psychological universe from the comparatively innocuous Victorian pornography of flagellation and submission to take one example. Society is confronted with a challenge and menace it probably faces for the first time.

Those who have contributed to the evidence presented in this book should be neither deterred nor surprised when they are criticised and attacked from many quarters. Findings and views that may lead to the imposition of fresh social constraints are bound to meet with opposition. But it may well be that when the factual evidence presented has been extended and refined, those who make and disseminate the uncensored video films described here, will be seen by society to have no more right to freedom from interference than those engaged in the manufacture and the sale of heroin, cocaine, dextroamphetamine, LSD and other drugs of addiction. For they do not merely endanger the mental health of a growing minority of young people; by generating crime and corruption on a large scale they threaten the very fabric of society. This book presents prima facie evidence that the overt sale and dissemination of video films that portray the morbid and macabre forms of violence exemplified in the Appendices and the exposure of a growing proportion of children to their influence constitute maladies of a similar character.

2 Television Violence and Children

Graham Melville-Thomas

Introduction

Before turning to investigate the possible effects of video violence on the young, it is appropriate to pay regard to the great deal of research that has already been carried out on television violence. The investigations have been extensive and the format variable. It would be quite impossible to deal with all the research here, but we hope sufficient representative background information will be presented in this chapter to underline the fact that although all the work quoted in this chapter is about television violence, the principle is the same with regard to the effects of video violence. If the previous research findings with regard to the effects of viewing television violence can be believed, it is logical to presume that the effects will be even stronger following the viewing of some of the more extreme violence portrayed in the so called 'video nasties'. To begin with we need to consider the general aspects of aggression, violence and the screen.

Effects of Media Violence on the Viewer

Aggression is usually defined as behaviour intended to injure a person or object either physically or verbally. The key word is that of intent. A distinction has been made by psychologists such as Pervin (1973), between hostile aggression where the sole aim is to injure, and instrumental aggression where certain rewards other than the victim's suffering (e.g. power, wealth and status) are the object of the behaviour. Violence would come under the first of these forms of aggression in that the sole aim is the suffering of the victim. The effects of viewing media violence may be seen as falling into three main categories:

1 The learning of aggression.
2 The increased arousal effect.
3 Desensitisation.

1 The Learning of Aggression

According to Social Learning Theory the child may copy acts of aggression, as seen through the media, which now forms such a large part of childhood experience. In Britain over ninety per cent of households own a television set and this is watched for an average of twenty-five hours a week. The fact that in Britain and the United States, television shows a violent scene every sixteen minutes and a murder every thirty minutes has caused much concern and many people believe the mass media play a much greater part in the teaching of aggressive behaviour and attitudes than is commonly realised.

Some professional and lay opinions were expressed during the 1970s advocating the reduction in the amount of violent content in fictional drama programmes. These views were largely supported by the experimental literature at that time which indicated a positive causal relationship between watching portrayals of violence on television and aggressive behaviour in individual viewers (Liebert and Baron, 1972), and by the reviews concerning the effects of media violence in society generally (Drabman and Thomas, 1974; Lefkowitz et al., 1977).

The question of whether violence portrayed through the mass media leads to increased interpersonal aggression has been a burning issue not only with social psychologists, but with the whole of Western society for a number of years. However there is also a danger of making a scapegoat of the media for all the violence in society. Violence as a social phenomenon is a complex issue and there are many variables involved with no one factor solely responsible for the increase in violence in recent years. At the same time there has been a growth of strong evidence to suggest that televised violence does play an important and contributory part in the learning of aggression (Parke et al., 1977; Berkowitz, 1974).

2 The Increased Arousal Effect

Filmed violence may also elicit aggressive behaviour by increasing the level of arousal in a viewer. Recordings of physiological data by galvanic skin response and heart rate have indicated much greater degrees of emotional arousal when children of four and five years of age view violent rather than non-violent television programmes (Osborn and Endsley, 1971). Speisman, Lazarus, Mordkoff and Davidson (1964) described how adults too show increased heart rate and GSR while watching violent scenes, and this emotional arousal enhanced the probability of aggressive behaviour especially if the individual is already angry or frustrated.

3 Desensitisation

It has also been found that while young children are emotionally aroused by watching violence, the strength of the arousal decreases with repeated exposure to displays of violence (Cline, Croft and Courrier, 1973). It is possible that the emotional blunting produced by continual exposure to filmed violence may affect the way a viewer will respond to real-life aggression (Thomas, Horton, Lippincott and Drabman, 1977). For example, the speed and willingness with which a viewer might intervene in a fist fight or respond to a victim's suffering may be decreased by watching scenes of violence.

Violence on television could also indirectly increase the likelihood of aggressive behaviour by reducing the restraints that one naturally imposes on aggressive impulses. These restraints, such as guilt, fear of retaliation, and disapproval by others, may be weakened by observing the aggression of others with no undesirable effects (Doob and Wood, 1972).

Many analyses of violence in society and its relationship to media violence have been based on field studies, while other research has been specifically aimed at measuring the immediate effects upon the viewer under laboratory conditions. One of the earliest of these assessments was by Berger (1962). He arranged for subjects to watch through a one-way screen the effects of giving simulated (not real) electric shocks to another subject sitting behind the screen. The experiment 'volunteer' was told to continue giving increasing voltages in spite of the obvious (but please note, simulated) pain effects in the recipient. What Berger demonstrated so effectively was the speed with which the average man can be desensitised or hardened sufficiently to carry out pain-inflicting actions he would not otherwise do. Berger's work has been the subject of a television programme, and effectively demonstrated how normal inhibitions can be lost under those experimental conditions.

The effects of viewing violent film on television have been investigated by Nias *et al*. (1979). He noted that up to that date over two hundred studies had been reported on the effects of witnessing violence in various ways, and added that almost all of these had indicated an increase in subsequent aggression. In spite of this evidence the authors point out how many commentators including film producers and academics rejected the conclusions. Against results of carefully conducted scientific experiments such critics would dismiss the studies as being of a trivial and too artificial nature, stating that in their view the methods and setting of the experiments were divorced from every day behaviour.

Eysenck and Nias (1978) and Nias (1979) emphasised the value of traditional scientific methods to test and evaluate theories, rather than setting out to collect data from field surveys or experimental field studies or individual cases. Their book summarises a large number of psychological research projects in their chapter on Laboratory Experiments. One of these

(Thomas *et al.*, 1977) explores the hypothesis that exposure to violence in the context of television drama decreases subjects' emotional responsivity to portrayals of real-life aggression. Emotional responses, as in other similar research, were measured continuously throughout sessions by changes in skin resistance. Two groups were examined; one of eight- to ten-year-old children, and another of adults (college students). In both age groups there were experimental and control groups. The study set out to consider whether exposure to television violence reduced viewers' responsivity to violence in general.

The immediate reactions during viewing were estimated by using skin electrodes placed on the finger. This is a well-tried method of detecting any rise and fall in anxiety levels through skin conductance. Participants were also asked to respond to a questionnaire. Naturally the film content and questionnaires varied with the two age groups.

The results of the two controlled experiments added strength to the argument that repeated observation of violent acts in dramatic television programmes can result in the blunting of viewers' emotional sensitivity to similar aggressive actions. It is important, the authors emphasise, that real life aggression film was used rather than fantasy violence. They concluded that in general their findings supported the suspicion 'that the excessive display of violence on television may be contributing to a population becoming increasingly inured to violence'.

Two Theories of Aggression

(a) Catharsis

The effects of observing violence are complex, and as stated they may operate in several ways, for example by teaching aggressive styles of behaviour, by increasing arousal or by desensitising people to violence. The Catharsis theory of aggression states that aggression is a drive, either innate or frustration produced, and as such its expression should lead to a reduction in the intensity of the aggressive feeling. If this is true, the watching of filmed violence on television should reduce the viewers' drive for aggression.

Feshbach (1961), for example, showed that students who were disappointed or vexed were less aggressive after they had seen an aggressive film than they were after viewing a neutral film. However his sample of 'normal' students who were rated as not disappointed but rather contented and who were shown an aggressive film, were later found to be more aggressive than similar students who were shown a neutral film. Feshbach concluded that watching aggressive films may have a cathartic effect on those in *a matching emotional state*, but would have a stimulating effect on those who during the viewing were in a neutral or non-aggressive state of mind.

(b) Social Learning Theory

Social Learning Theory rejects the idea of aggression as an instinct or frustration-produced drive and suggests that aggression is no different from any other learned response. It proposes that aggression can be learned through observation and imitation and the more often it is reinforced the more likely it is to occur.

A number of studies have shown an increase in potential aggression due to the viewing of violence. For example, Bandura, Ross and Ross (1963) divided three- to six-year-old children into three experimental groups and one control group. The children watched either a film showing models being aggressive to a variety of objects or a neutral film. The children were then allowed to play with a number of different objects including the ones they had just seen eliciting aggressive responses. Bandura *et al.* found that the experimental groups on average showed about twice as much 'aggression' as the control group which had seen no violence at all. They found an increase not only in the number of aggressive acts similar to those watched, but also in many other types of aggressive acts which were unrelated in character. The same kind of variation in aggressive behaviour of specific and non-specific nature was seen in the case studies reported in Chapter 7 of this book, where disturbances of behaviour followed violent video viewing.

Within the experimental groups Bandura *et al.* found that the group who watched the live model showed a larger number of imitative acts while the group who had watched the cartoon showed a larger number of non-imitative acts. Bandura, Ross and Ross conclude that **the more unlike the model is to a human being the weaker the tendency to copy the model's behaviour**. This view could be important when considering how much of media violence is directly portrayed by the human model. It is even more realistically portrayed in the violent videos.

Finally, the impact of learning from filmed violence has been assessed using measures of more realistic forms of aggression than is normally obtained in the relatively restricted environment of the laboratory situation. Berkowitz *et al.* (1977) conducted experiments on the reactions of juvenile delinquents to filmed violence. Their results extended the generality of the earlier findings obtained with university students. An extreme form of delinquent reaction is mentioned in a case in 1973 when a young woman was assaulted by a gang of youths in Boston who poured petrol on her and then set it alight. Police investigators were convinced that the youths had copied the action from a very similar scene shown only the day before in a popular television crime programme.

Research Studies in Britain

In the early 1970s the Columbia Broadcasting System of the USA funded a major UK study of the effects on boys of long term exposure to television violence. The study was directed by Dr William Belson of the Survey Research Centre, an organisation specialising in testing and developing research techniques and in mass media research. In an extended technique development phase of the work, the Centre developed strategies for investigating causal hypotheses, built and tested techniques for measuring personal involvement in violent behaviour and long-term exposure to the different kinds of television violence, constructed measures of desensitisation and of various attitudes to the use of violence. These measures were used in a study based on 1,565 London boys aged 13 to 16 years. The sample members were divided into the more and the less exposed to television violence. The two groups were then subjected to massive matching in terms of variables (a pool of 217 variables was used) associated with violent behaviour, including childhood pre-disposition towards being violent as an adolescent.

The results gave very strong support to the following hypotheses:

1 Long-term exposure to television violence increases substantially the degree to which adolescent boys engage in serious violence themselves.
2 This effect is greater with respect to exposure to programmes that present violence in the context of close personal relationships, that show violence being done by 'good guys' or in the maintenance of law and order, that are realistic in presentation, that show gratuitous violence, that present violent westerns.
3 The serious violence that is increased by television tends to be unskilled and spontaneous in character.
4 The increase in violent behaviour produced by exposure to television is not accompanied by attitude changes at the conscious level.

The recommendations made were that the amount of violence presented on television be sharply reduced, especially violence of the kind most associated with the production of adolescent violence; that a monitoring service be set up to establish and to report upon the extent and the nature of violence presented on television. The results and the methods of this enquiry are given in detail in *Television Violence and the Adolescent Boy* by William Belson (Gower Publishing Company).

Apart from the study by Belson, there has been little research in Britain in recent years. Holden (1982) has published a review of British research entitled *The Effects of Television on Children: A Review of Research*. Emmett (1983) has also published a survey for the BBC on *The Portrayal of Violence in Television Programmes*. In this, he suggests a fairly weak causal link between television violence and children's behaviour, and concludes that 'exposure to constant scenes of violence may blunt the emotions and sensibilities of the viewer, so that he comes to accept violence as commonplace' (Emmett, 1983).

American Studies

Most of the research into the effects of television violence has been done in the United States of America, where there have been two reports to the US Senate with an interval of ten years between the two reports. The National Coalition on Television Violence (USA) has listed 700 studies and reports which have been produced by a wide range of academic disciplines including paediatrics, psychology, sociology, education and child development and child psychiatry. These wide ranging surveys are reported as covering over 100,000 people. A review editorial by Rothenberg (1983) dealt with 'The Role of Television in Shaping the Attitudes of Children', and quoted an earlier work by Murray entitled *Television and Youth: 25 years of Research and Controversy*.

Early concern about the growing violence in society led to the first of the US Government Commissions. This was prompted by the assassinations of John and Robert Kennedy and Martin Luther King, and was set up by President Johnson to investigate violence in all its aspects. The committee included lawyers, and politicians and one psychiatrist, and after referring to various experts in their specialist areas it produced its findings after eighteen months in the 'National Commission on the Causes and Prevention of Violence, 1969'.

Out of its fifteen volumes the Commission produced two volumes dealing with television violence and its effects (Baker and Ball, 1969; Briand, 1969). They reported an increase of one hundred per cent in the number of crimes of violence, including homicide, rape and robbery with assault in the United States of America during the previous decade, but were sceptical about the direct influence of screened violence. Following public concern, President Johnson also set up a second team to investigate pornography. Beginning their enquiry in 1967, they published their results in the US Commission on Obscenity and Pornography, 1970.

It has been pointed out (Cline, 1974; Eysenck and Nias, 1978) that the constitution of both these American Commissions contained mostly persons with liberal attitudes who held mainly anti-censorship views. Most of them found it difficult to believe in the possibility of harmful effects on children and young persons.

It is, of course, widely recognised that the methodological problems of research into the effects of media violence are very great. Effects are complex and are determined by interactions between programme attributes and the personality characteristics of the viewer. In addition there is the variation in the general cultural milieu of approval or disapproval. The findings of these two early Commissions, so far as the effects of media violence were concerned, were worded in such a way that there was an impression of conflict and uncertainty in the presentation of the research conclusions. An overall impression of 'no harm can be done' emerged.

It took a whole decade before the evidence was again sifted and reviewed in America. This time the focus was more specifically on the possible effects of television violence upon viewers, and the summary conclusions were in sharp contrast to the indeterminate findings of the US Commissions ten years earlier.

Under the auspices of the US National Institute for Mental Health, the report, *Television and Behaviour: Ten Years of Scientific Progress and Implications for the Eighties* (1982), was presented to the US Government. One of its authors, Dr D. Pearl, said **'We have come to a unanimous conclusion that there is a causal relationship between television violence and real life violence.'** (Pearl *et al.*, 1982.)

What has been responsible for this marked change of opinion over a ten year interval? Have the conclusions swung from one direction to another because of a change in the researchers' approach? Or could it be that ten years of media violence has slowly but surely desensitised a vast viewing public of adults and children which has now become apparent to researchers? At the same time the part played by a general shift in the social and economic climate both in America and the United Kingdom has to be considered. Factors of change in society over the past ten years include substantial increases in family breakdown, unemployment, family violence and sex-abuse of children which have come to the attention of the public as never before. Each of these factors compound each other and there is clearly no point in looking for a single predominant cause. Nevertheless, the importance of the part played by media violence has had to be evaluated.

Evidence also comes from the National Coalition on Television Violence USA. Its Chairman, Dr Radecki, in reporting to the US House of Representatives Sub-Committee on Telecommunications in October 1981, considered that his units' research, taking into account the various **possible** causes of real-life violence, regarded media violence as a significant contribution to real life violence in American society.

Other research showed that adolescents were just as strongly affected as children (Radecki, 1981).

The effect of eliminating or reducing the experience of television violence by juniors has not been studied to such a great extent. One survey of middle class adult males by R. Gormais found a significant reduction in 'hurtful behaviour around the home' during a single week when violent programmes were eliminated from viewing. More such studies are clearly needed over longer periods of time and should involve children and adolescents.

One of the factors contributing towards violence in society which can be controlled by public pressure is media violence. We do not have to have more violence on our television programmes, nor do we have to allow the circulation of video programmes purposely setting out to highlight violence, sadism and pornography. Each society must decide for itself what it chooses to allow, but this choice should be based upon knowledge gained from the investigations and research carried out into the effects on children of their exposure to scenes of violence.

The issue of co-operation between media producers and those responsible for scientific inquiry is of paramount importance in planning future patterns of television programmes which contain scenes of violence and sex.

In a review of how the media and social science research can be co-ordinated, Alan Wortzel of the American Broadcasting Companies Inc. writes that scientific research may have a meaningful and effective impact on television, but he also quotes Eli Rubinstein (1978) who talks about the basic dichotomy between the approaches of the social scientist and the media producers, both of whom tend to give contrasting answers to what they think of as 'good for the public'.

'The Social Scientist,' says Rubinstein, 'may make too sweeping recommendations . . . with no understanding of the pressures and necessities of the production.' Herein lies the conflict in deciding what should be screened, bearing in mind that children often watch what is not primarily intended for them. After the disclosures of the NIMH Report in 1982, Rubinstein considered that the continued emphasis on televised violence might mask a larger issue, namely the total effect of television as an educating agency. As stated earlier, the main 'educative' experience in childhood today is not schooling but the media, in terms of total hours spent on average throughout childhood (Greenfield, 1984).

A similar conclusion was reached in an article in the Journal of the American Medical Association (March 1985). This reported on the results of a research programme into the effects of television upon young people. It noted that by the time that the average American student graduates from college he will have spent 18,000 hours watching television. This compares with only 11,000 hours spent in the classroom.

Children's Choice

By far the greatest part of children's viewing is of adult television and the limited degree to which there is monitoring of children's television viewing is carried out by the parents themselves (National Children's Bureau summary of the literature, 1982). There is some multi-factorial research on the choices of viewing by children of the media. This work is currently being carried out by the American Paediatric Association and includes such separate issues as eating habits and commercials, diet and obesity, as well as the factor of television violence and children's behaviour.

On a positive aspect of viewing it has been reported that children, given the choice would prefer watching children's programmes specially designed for them rather than the adult material to which they are more frequently exposed during the day.

One study looked at the selection of material viewed by children in a

Canadian hospital and showed a higher viewing rate of the hospital's specially-made closed circuit television channel, when compared with the adult media (D. N. Gutentag, 1983).

Gutentag found that 83% of the younger children in his sample chose the hospital closed circuit television irrespective of the length of stay in hospital. The author points out that much of what children view during the day is adult-orientated, and he asks why since so many children watch television there is not a channel for children? Day-time schedules in the UK also contain a significant proportion of programmes for adult audiences unsuitable for younger children (five to eleven years).

Television and the Family

Some research has included information about the circumstances under which families view their television screens (Rubenstein, 1983). One investigation in the USA has shown that parents do not usually watch television with their children. Studies have shown that although much parental concern was expressed about the level of sex and violence on television, there was at the same time a relatively low level of parental control over what was being watched. This point of parental control is particularly important for young children. When, for example, a four- or five-year-old who has seen little television sees a violent film and asks the penetratingly simple question 'Why are they fighting?', the parent's presence or absence may be of vital importance. How they respond and answer is equally important. The absence of the parent or the lack of parental involvement or interaction is, according to some studies, all too prevalent. This is unfortunate since other work has revealed that sensible parental intervention and comment can help the child to deal with the negative and violent aspects of the programme, in a more positive way. Some television programmes that contain scenes which may disturb a child emphasise the importance of parents watching programmes with their children.

Effects of Modelling   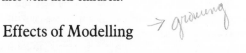 → growing

Quite apart from the effects of desensitising children and young persons to violence and increasing levels of arousal, television violence can have the more specific effect of children modelling themselves on certain media characters (Cline *et al.*, 1973).

Children are known to be great imitators and in the field of social learning are regularly picking up models of behaviour from the screen. How and to what extent they are influenced is still being considered. Cline, Croft and Courrier (1973) argue that television violence has the potential to reduce the restraints of 'conscience and concern' through the desensitising processes, and at the same time through the effects of modelling it may provide clear and suggestive examples of how violent acts may be committed. This relatively weak potential of violent television programmes has become much stronger in the violent videos and a few cases of direct copying of a crime as shown on the video have been reported, including serious crimes such as murder and rape.

Attitudes of growing indifference and unconcern for the victim, side by side with a higher level of personal violence in society can, according to Cline *et al.* (1973), hardly be surprising. Their research concerned two groups of children, with previously high and low levels of exposure to television violence. Forty-one children between the ages of 7 and 14 were carefully monitored in their study. Through the use of physiological measurements they found that the highly exposed children 'responded' far less when shown moderately violent film, than did the low exposure group. They comment on the serious effect of generalised desensitisation that may follow the regular viewing of media violence. However, because of the limited numbers and the use of only one film depicting violence, the authors express caution about making inappropriate conclusions out of their findings.

This type of study, with its acknowledged limitations, does nevertheless prove the existence of measurable differences in child responses which vary according to the amount of television previously viewed. It also draws attention to the imitative behaviour which may be carried out by children as a result of watching television. The fact that young children will imitate the aggressive behaviour of filmed models in play, has been shown by Bandura *et al.* (1963) and the lasting nature of such an effect has been illustrated by Kniveton (1973). Criticism has been levelled at these studies because the indices of aggression were not sufficiently real, that is; the aggressive actions were towards toy material and the circumstances of the aggression were not real. A further study by Kniveton and Stephenson (1975) set out to study interpersonal aggression between children, and how this might be influenced by the pre-viewing of a film portraying a violent relationship between two children. From 48 middle class and 48 working class boys in the first year of their primary schooling the results indicated a different outcome according to social class. The working class boys were more 'assertive'. Very few of the aggressive acts were copied in any detail, but the inhibiting effects of adults in authority being present, were also acknowledged.

Many of these studies attempting to discover whether children have a 'copy-cat' response to things seen on television, and if so, how and to what extent, have run into methodological difficulties, and these are clearly acknowledged. In spite of these difficulties however, the studies raise many important issues and demonstrate that, with certain reservations, effects of a *short term nature* can be demonstrated. Similar work continues, and should continue because the experience of television in children's lives seems to be increasing.

Personality and the Media Viewer

The fact that children will vary in their responses to television violence has always been acknowledged but, according to Eysenck and Nias (1978), since individual differences are so marked and universal they should be taken into account far more in future research into assessment of responses to the filmed portrayal of violence and pornography. Only a small number of researchers such as Gunter and Furnham (1983) and Gunter (1983) have so far concentrated on this issue. In doing so they also point out the heterogeneous nature of the effects of watching violent television portrayals and of the need to take this variable into account.

On finding evidence from previous research that greater viewing of violent television material occurred in those who had the stronger predispositions towards aggression, Gunter (1983) set out to investigate the relationship between the personality of the viewer and the material viewed. He concluded that from the evidence reviewed, individuals who are more attracted to aggression seem themselves to be more drawn to watching violent material. McIntyre and Teevan (1972) studying attitudes and viewing, found that adolescents who approved of violence in the media were also more likely to behave in a deviant and aggressive manner towards others. Aggressive boys, who were more likely to be involved in fighting, hitting a teacher or using a knife or gun to get something from another person, were found to favour the violent programmes, more than the non-aggressive boys (Friedman and Johnson, 1972). It may be, therefore, that the relationship between the viewing of violent scenes on television and aggressive behaviour is not a one-way causal relationship. It is possible that those who are already predisposed towards aggressive behaviour enjoy watching aggression. The effect may be cumulative.

The study by Friedman and Johnson (1972) was based on correlation analyses and like a number of other experiments has drawn attention to the mounting evidence for the association between violent content on television and aggression and deviance in real life in young people and children.

An opposite view is expressed by Howitt and Cumberbatch (1975) whose review of the research literature led them to conclude that it has 'shown effectively that the mass media – as far as it is possible to tell using social scientific methodologies – do not serve to amplify the level of violence in society.'

However, one may fairly doubt the value of their assessment and use of 'social scientific methodologies' in the light of Cumberbatch's more recent criticism of the findings of the research (summarised in the next chapter) of the National Viewers' Survey. Cumberbatch claimed that the figures given for the number of children who claimed to have seen violent videos were implausible or 'could not be true' on the grounds that most people are not aware of the 'video nasty flood' or that 'it's hard to find a video nasty' (*The*

Guardian, 25 April 1984). However, unless, or until, genuine counter evidence is supplied, this and other figures obtained from the National Viewers' Survey must stand, subject to interpretation in the light of research design, sample size, definition of 'video nasty' and the timing of the survey (*before* the parliamentary debates concerning the Video Recordings Bill).

Cumberbatch also challenged the results of the National Viewers' Survey on the grounds that children are unreliable respondents. Problems of reliability and recall were acknowledged and discussed in the Research Report (Part 2, paragraph c40) and the research methodology designed to overcome these was outlined. Cumberbatch carried out a small piece of research in which he tested a different variable and then used this as grounds to attack the reliability of our research. He gave five classes of 11-year-olds the questionnaire used in the National Viewers' Survey but with slight changes in film titles. They found that 68% of the children claimed to have seen films which did not exist. But the bogus titles were very similar to actual titles (e.g. *Zombies from Beyond Space*; *Vampire Holocaust*). They were therefore testing *title recall* rather than reliability as such. Their findings were used to claim that children are unreliable, but this has not actually been demonstrated. Unlike the critics, the original investigation used a variety of tests including class discussion to check how much children knew of the *content* of the films which they claimed to have seen.

Discussion

Although many studies have proven an association between exposure to violence and behaviour, none has so far been able to provide unequivocal proof of causality.

As children grow up they tend to spend more time in front of their television sets and more of the programmes contain elements of dramatic violence, which is perhaps mainly meant for adults but possibly seen just as much or more by children. The accumulative effects on all types of young personality can still only be conjectured, but research to date strongly indicates associations between aggressive type, aggressive behaviour and viewing violent material on television.

The main medium for films in the past has been the television and the cinema, but we now have another medium namely the videotape in which the violent content can go far beyond that previously shown on television.

The research presented in this book may be regarded in one way as a continuity of previous extensive research into television and cinema violence, but in other ways it is different; firstly, because of the nature of the content under consideration which is far more realistic and sadistic, and secondly because of the accessibility of video to children and adolescents who may view it with or without their parents' knowledge or approval. The violent content of television has been fully researched, and all previous findings lay a basis for what is to be considered here, so far as the new wave of extraordinary violent and explicit videotapes is concerned. According to John Heinz of the US Senate (Heinz, 1983), any doubt about the profound impact of television viewing on children has been dispelled by the wide-ranging evidence and the comprehensive study by the National Institute for Mental Health (1982).

The finding in the NIMH Report that, after ten years of uncertainty, violence on the screen does have negative effects on children, forms a sobering prelude to national reaction and policy-making regarding the new dimension of violence available in the home on the videotape.

Summary

Since in principle it is appropriate for research to be built upon what is already known in related areas, we have in this chapter taken into account an overview (albeit incomplete) of some of the major studies already carried out in the field of television violence.

Since it is the same factor of violence in both television and the video which concerns us, we approach the problem of assessment consciously continuing the flow of previous research carried out with regard to the mass media. In view of the scope of our enquiry, we have been primarily concerned with those studies which have looked at the relationships between violent content in television programmes and young viewers. The possible ways in which a viewer may be influenced by media violence are outlined, and reference is made to two theoretical approaches, namely Catharsis and Social Learning Theory. The paucity of literature on personality factors has been noted by previous researchers. This is an important factor which is at present inadequately researched.

Two Commissions in the United States of America together with other surveys are summarised, and some of the laboratory experiments studying the immediate effects of viewing horror or violent material are described.

The weight of evidence in the literature examined points to filmed violence having a stimulating rather than cathartic effect upon the great majority of children.

Acknowledgments

I would like to thank those members of the Working Party who offered helpful comments on the first draft of this chapter. I am especially indebted to Dr William Belson who kindly summarised his work for us which is included in this chapter under *Research Studies in Britain*. I am indebted to Mr Kenneth Howkins, Senior Lecturer at Hertfordshire College of Higher

Education and Dr Howard Davies for the critique of Cumberbatch on page 19.

References

BAKER and BALL (1969) 'Television Violence and Its Effects'. National Commission on the Causes and Prevention of Violence, US Government Printing Office.

BANDURA, A., ROSS, D. and ROSS, S. A. (1963) 'Imitation of film-mediated aggressive models', *Journal of Abnormal and Social Psychology*, Vol. 66, No. 1, pp. 3–11.

BERGER, S. M. (1962) 'Conditioning through vicarious instigation', *Psychology Review*, Vol. 69, No. 45a, p. 466.

BERKOWITZ, L. (1974) 'Some determinants of impulsive aggression role of mediated associations with re-inforcements for aggression'. *Psychological Review*, 81, pp. 165–76.

BOZZUTO, J. C. (1975) 'Cinematic Neurosis Following *The Exorcist*', *Journal of Nervous and Mental Diseases*.

BRIAND (1969) 'Television Violence and Its Effects'. National Commission on the Causes and Prevention of Violence, US Government Printing Office.

CLINE, V. B., CROFT, R. G. and COURRIER, S. (1973) 'Desensitisation of Children to Television Violence', *Journal of Personality and Social Psychology*, Vol. 27, No. 3, pp. 360–365.

DOOB, A. N. and WOOD, L. E. (1972) 'Catharsis and aggression: effects of annoyance and retaliation on aggressive behaviour'. *Journal of Personal and Social Psychology*, 22 May, pp. 156–62.

DRABMAN, R. S. and THOMAS, M. H. (1974) 'Does media violence increase children's tolerance of real life aggression?'. *Developmental Psychology*, 10, pp. 418–21.

DUNN, G. (1974) *Television and the Pre-school Child*. IBA.

EMMETT (1979) *The Portrayal of Violence in Television Programmes*. BBC.

EYSENCK, H. J. and NIAS, D. K. B. (1978) *Sex, Violence and the Media*. Temple Smith.

FESHBACH, S. (1961) 'The stimulating versus cathartic effects of a vicarious aggressive activity'. *Journal of Abnormal and Social Psychology*, 63, September, pp. 381–5.

FRIEDMAN, H. and JOHNSON, R. L. (1972) 'Mass media use and aggression', a pilot study in CORNSTOCK, G. A. and RUBINSTEIN, E. A. (eds) *Television and Adolescent Aggressiveness*. US Government Printing Office.

GERBNER, G. (1972) 'Violence in television drama: trends and symbolic functions', in CORNSTOCK, G. A. and RUBINSTEIN, E. A. (eds) *Television and Social Behaviour Vol. 1 – Media Content and Control*. US Government Printing Office.

GUNTER, B. (1983) 'Do aggressive people prefer violent television?', *Bulletin of the British Psychology Society*, No. 36, pp. 166–8.

GUNTER, B. and FURNHAM, A. (1983) 'Personality and the Perception of television violence', *Personality and Individual Differences*, Vol. 4, No. 3, pp. 315–321.

GUTTENTAG, D. N. *et al.* (1983) 'Daytime television viewing by hospitalised children: the effect of alternative programming', *Paediatrics*, April 71(4), pp. 62–5.

HEINZ, J. (1983) 'National Leadership for Children's Television', *American Psychologist*, July, pp. 817–19.

HILL, C. *et al.* (1984) *Video Violence and Children: Children's Viewing Patterns and Parental Attitudes in England and Wales*. Report of a Parliamentary Group Video Enquiry (Part 2).

HOLDEN, H. (1982) *The Effects of Television on Children: A review of the research.* National Children's Bureau.

HOWITT and CUMBERBATCH (1975) *Mass Media Violence and Society.* Elek Science.

KNIVETON, B. H. (1973) 'The effect of rehearsal delay on long-term imitation of filmed aggression', *British Journal of Psychology*, 64(2), pp. 259–65.

KNIVETON, B. H. and STEPHENSON, G. M. (1975) 'The effects of an aggressive film model on social class and working class boys', *Journal of Child Psychology and Psychiatry*, Vol. 16, pp. 301–13.

LEFKOWITZ, M. M., ERON, L. D., WALDER, L. O. and HUESMANN, L. R. *Growing up to be violent. A longitudinal study of the Development of Aggression.* New York: Pergamon Press Ltd.

LEIBERT, R. M. and BARON, R. A. (1971) 'Short term effects of televised aggression on children's aggressive behaviour'. Paper presented at the meeting of the American Psychological Association, Washington DC, September.

MCINTYRE, J. and TEEVAN, J. (1972) 'Television violence and deviant behaviour' in CORNSTOCK, G. A. and RUBINSTEIN, E. A. (eds) *Television and Social Behaviour Vol. 3 – Television and Adolescent Aggressiveness.* US Government Printing Office.

MURRAY, J. P. *Television and Youth: 25 Years of Research and Controversy.* Boys Town Centre for the Study of Youth Development, Nebraska, USA.

NIAS, D. K. (1979) 'The classification and correlates of children's academic and recreational interests'. *Journal of Child Psychology and Psychiatry.* 20 (1), January, pp. 73–9.

NIAS, D. K. B. (1979) 'Desensitisation and Media Violence' *Journal of Psychosomatic Research*, Vol. 23, pp. 363–367.

OSBORNE, D. K. and ENDSLEY, R. C. (1971) 'Emotional reactions of young children to TV violence'. *Child Development*, 42 March, pp. 321–31.

PARKE, R. D., BERKOWITZ, L., LEYENS, J. P., WEST, S. and SEBASTIAN, R. J. (1977) 'Film violence and aggression. A field experimental analysis' in KERKOWITZ, L. (ed.) *Advances in Experimental Social Psychology, Vol. 10.* New York: Academic Press.

PEARL, D., BOUTHILET, L. and LAZAR, J. (1982) *Television and Behaviour: Ten Years of Scientific Progress and Implications for the Eighties* (Vols. 1 and 2). US Government Printing Office.

RADECKI (October 1981) Extract of US House of Representatives. Hearing: Sub Committee on Telecommunications.

ROTHENBERG, M. B. (1983) 'The Role of Television in Shaping the Attitudes of Children', *Journal of the American Academy of Child Psychiatry.*

RUBINSTEIN, E. A. (1983) 'Television and Behaviour', research conclusions of the 1982 NIMH Report and their policy implications. *American Psychologist.*

SPEISMAN, J. C., LAZARUS, R. S., DAVISON, L. *et al.* (1964) 'Experimental analysis of a film used as a threatening stimulus' *Journal of Consultant Psychology.* 28, February, pp. 23–33.

THOMAS, M. H., HORTON, R. W., LIPPINCOTT, E. C. and DRABMAN, R. S. (1977) 'Desensitisation to portrayals of real live aggression as a function of exposure to television violence'. *Journal of Personality and Social Psychology*, 35, pp. 450–58.

ZUCKERMAN, D. M. and ZUCKERMAN, B. S. (1985) 'Television's impact on children', *Paediatrics*, Vol. 75, No. 2.

3 Historical Background to the Video Enquiry

Clifford Hill

The comparatively new social phenomenon of the unrestricted availability for home viewing of uncensored and unclassified films on videotape was first brought to the attention of Parliament by Mr Gareth Wardell, Labour MP for Gower. In the autumn of 1982 he introduced a Private Members Bill in the Commons on this subject. Although the Bill was subsequently withdrawn, Mr Wardell took the opportunity of describing to the House some of the scenes of horrific violence displayed in these video films and appealed for controls in order to protect young children from seeing them.

From the middle of 1982 reports began appearing in the press linking the viewing of violent video films with violent behaviour and indicating that ultra-violent videos were having a damaging effect upon the lives of young people. In the New Year of 1983 the subject was discussed at the Child and Family Welfare Committee – an all-party Parliamentary committee chaired by Mrs Jill Knight MP, Vice Chairman Dr John Blackburn MP.

With the rise in public awareness of a possible source of particular danger to children, the free availability of all types of video films was being widely discussed both in the press and among Members of Parliament. A meeting for Members of both Houses and all political parties together with senior representatives of the Churches to discuss the situation was called by Viscount Ingleby to take place at a room in the House of Lords in May 1983. A few days before the meeting was due to take place the General Election was announced and the meeting was postponed until the new House could assemble.

The meeting took place on 27 June 1983. Lord Nugent of Guildford took the chair and following a wide-ranging discussion it was decided to sponsor an Enquiry, privately funded by individuals and Churches, to produce factual evidence of the situation existing in the country. This was intended to give guidance to Members of both Houses on a social situation that was giving concern and upon which there appeared to be very little reliable evidence. After studying the evidence produced by the Enquiry, Members would then introduce proposed legislation if that were found to be appropriate. I was asked to direct the Enquiry and together with Mr Raymond

Johnston I was to produce an outline of research proposals that would be considered by a meeting one month later.

The meeting on 27 June clashed with the Annual Assembly of the Methodist Church so that none of its leaders who had agreed to attend the earlier meeting were available. They were represented by a lecturer from Oxford Polytechnic who volunteered his services and offered to host the research in his department (the Television Research Unit, TRU). This offer was accepted gladly.

Working Party

The second meeting of the Sponsors on 26 July 1983 considered the research proposals and decided to implement them by the setting up of an academic Working Party under the chairmanship of the Lord Swinfen and Dr Brian Mawhinney MP. (Dr Mawhinney subsequently withdrew due to pressure of other work.) A list of names for the Working Party was approved and Mr Johnston agreed to convene the first meeting. He would not, however, be a member of the Working Party as he was part of a campaign organisation.

It was decided to keep the academic Working Party entirely separate from the sponsoring body and from any political or campaigning influence. The Working Party were to be left completely free to pursue their task of producing empirical evidence which was intended to be of the most trustworthy academic nature and each individual on the Working Party was appointed with this in mind. The members were:

The Lord Swinfen, JP, ARICS, Chairman
Dr Clifford Hill, MA, BD, PhD, Director of the Enquiry
Dr Howard Davis, BA, PhD, Media Sociologist, Edinburgh
Professor Peter Gray, MB, ChB, FRCP, DCH, Professor of Child Health, Cardiff
Dr Robert Holman, BA, PhD, former Professor of Social Administration, Community Worker, Bath
Mr Peter Liddelow, JP, Comprehensive School Deputy Headmaster, London
Dr Graham Melville-Thomas, MB, FRCPsych, DPM, Child Psychiatrist, Cardiff
Professor Andrew Sims, MD, FRCPsych, Professor of Psychiatry, University of Leeds
Mr Alec Taylor, BA, BAFTA, Video Consultant, London
Mrs Pat Wynnejones, BA, Cert of Ed, Lecturer in Education, London

Terms of Reference

The research for the Enquiry fell into three sections, each of which was to be pursued concurrently. The first section was to provide Members of Parliament with an overview of the current social, commercial and legal situation in Britain in regard to video films depicting scenes of explicit violence. The Enquiry was to investigate the phenomenon of violence not pornography and initially to provide a working definition of ultra-violent video films, to obtain information from the video industry in regard to the market, the geographical availability of these films, whether or not they were available to children and who were the distributors of these films. On the legal side the Enquiry would discover whether or not the ultra-violent video films were of such a nature as to render them liable to prosecution under the existing law, namely the Obscene Publications Act 1959. If that were so, were the police already acting against them, and was existing legislation sufficient to deal with the situation?

The second part of the Enquiry was to produce statistical data relating to films that had actually been seen by children and to compare this with such British Board of Film Censors' ratings given to the films or in the case of those video films with no ratings, to obtain from the film-makers or distributors their own assessment of their target audience. The objective was thus to produce empirical evidence of children's viewing patterns in relation to the suitability of the films seen. The Enquiry would also investigate the circumstances under which children were seeing video films and the views of a representative sample of parents. The objective of this was to reveal the social situation in the nation as a background to the consideration of a need for additional legislation.

The third part of the Enquiry was to deal with the effects upon children of their viewing scenes of violence in video films. Although this research would have an empirical basis it was recognised that this is a complex area where it is difficult to isolate variables and that the data thereby does not easily lend itself to statistical analysis. It was recognised that this part of the research would largely be based upon professional opinions, clinical experience and the collation and examination of case study data.

The composition of the Working Party had been formed with the wide-ranging objectives of the research in mind. In addition to the Working Party it was recognised that there would need to be a small full-time research team to work in close association and under the general direction of the Working Party. The team would be led by the Director.

Video Recordings Bill

The announcement in July 1983 by Mr Graham Bright of his intention to introduce a Bill to control the availability of video films was considered at the meeting on 26 July. It was decided to continue with the Enquiry on the grounds that the research would produce empirical evidence that would be invaluable in creating informed debates when the proposed legislation was considered. It was decided to make changes in the timetable of the research and to engage a larger research team in order to meet the Parliamentary timetable so that at least the empirical evidence of the current social and legal situation together with the data relating to children's viewing patterns of video films could be available for consideration during the debates on the Video Recordings Bill. This meant undertaking a six-month intensive piece of research with a Report available in the New Year or at least by March 1984 in time for the later stages of the Bill.

Work on the first section of the Enquiry was begun immediately, August 1983. It was the intention of the Working Party that the project concerning the investigation of children's viewing patterns would largely be carried out at Oxford but that other parts of the Enquiry would be based in London or in Cardiff or in Leeds University where members of the Working Party had academic bases. The work at Oxford commenced in mid-September but in the event was only based there for two months. It was intended that the investigation of children's viewing patterns and parental attitudes would largely be based upon data obtained from a sample survey of respondents using self-completed questionnaires. The children and their parents taking part in the survey were to be drawn from a sample of schools in all the 103 Local Education Authorities in England and Wales. Children in the sample would be of both sexes and all age groups. At a later stage it was decided not to use data from any children below the age of seven. The schools' sample was weighted for social geography and social class.

Practical problems

It was originally hoped to leave the schools project largely in the hands of the team at Oxford Polytechnic thus leaving the Director free to press on with other aspects of the Enquiry that were based elsewhere and to keep an overview of the whole research programme.

Within a few weeks, however, a number of problems arose with the work at Oxford. These were discussed with the Head of the Education Department and the Dean of the College both of whom advised relocating the research base. As there was no other department within the Polytechnic where the research could be continued, the Executive of the Sponsors decided to remove the research from Oxford. The college authorities were fully co-operative in the transfer of the research base. The Dean himself handed over some of the boxes of questionnaires, tapes and other research data pertaining to the Enquiry.

The Sponsors took offices in London with computer facilities and the academic Working Party engaged three additional researchers and a data analyst to strengthen the research team. The team was further strengthened by the appointment of Dr Geoffrey Nelson, Principal Lecturer in Sociology at Birmingham Polytechnic, who was engaged as consultant sociologist.

Interim Report

The timetable of the research provided for the publication of a Report at the earliest in the New Year of 1984. At the request of the sponsors, however, the Working Party agreed to produce an interim Report that would make some data available for the Commons Committee Stage of the Video Recordings Bill. The Working Party advised against publication of this Report but the Parliamentary Group decided to publish. They did so on the grounds that if the data were to be made available for the Commons Committee it should be available to the public.

Of necessity this interim Report used incomplete figures which made it vulnerable to misinterpretation and criticism although the Report stressed that the survey was not complete and that the figures were, therefore, provisional. No conclusions were offered but rather a series of questions were posed by the interim results of the children's data so far analysed.

Publicity

The amount of publicity given to this interim Report took everyone connected with the Enquiry by surprise. It was given full front-page treatment by most of the popular daily newspapers and it was featured on all radio and television news broadcasts. It was the subject of a great deal of commentary because it revealed that large numbers of schoolchildren were seeing video films of a particularly violent and horrific nature. Many of these video films could not legally be shown in a cinema even for adult entertainment. Thus there was revealed a social situation that was particularly disturbing for its possible effects upon children.

The level of public interest in the video issue meant that anything related to the Enquiry was now news-worthy. This inevitably gave occasion to those who were opponents of controls on home-viewing to attack the credibility of the research. Not only was the interim Report vulnerable due to its releasing of incomplete statistics but as soon as it became known that there had been problems within the research team resulting in staff changes and relocation of research base this provided a situation that was easily exploitable.

Neither the Sponsors nor the Working Party were aware of the strength of the forces opposed to the legal control of video films. A number of inaccurate press reports concerning the research began to appear that were damaging to the credibility of the research. A BBC reporter discovered that these were emanating from a sector of the video industry.

However, the sponsors decided upon a policy of no further public statements and the Working Party was instructed to leave all matters of public debate in the hands of the Parliamentary Group. They believed that the best answer to the critics would be the publication of the main Report, Part II, which would give the fully-completed survey and its analyses and would in fact broadly confirm the picture given in the Report Part I. They therefore refrained from further comment at this time. Their silence in the face of accusation concerning the reliability of the research, however, inevitably led to the suspicion of guilt that was not easy to dispel.

The academic Working Party, in fact, gave scant attention to the press reports and was content to leave such matters in the hands of the Parliamentary Group. On their part the Sponsors took the view that the Working Party was of such status and its work of such a standard that there was no need for any public defence. They believed that the quality of the research was such that once the full Report was published it would speak for itself. They therefore maintained a dignified silence and waited for the criticisms to abate!

Soon after the publication of the Report Part II lawyers representing some of the video film distributors made an application to the Attorney General citing Lord Nugent, Viscount Ingleby (Chairman and Vice Chairman of the Sponsors) and Lord Swinfen (Chairman of the Working Party) as being in contempt of Court in respect of the Report which contained synopses of some of the video films that were currently the subject of legal proceedings in various parts of the country. After due consideration the Attorney General rejected the allegations and refused to take any action against the three Peers. But if these complaints had been successful the Report would have had to have been withdrawn and its evidence would not have been available for the Parliamentary debates.

None of these matters was made public as the Sponsors did not want any publicity that might have detracted from the main issues during the period of the due process of Parliamentary consideration of the Video Recordings Bill.

Report Part II

The main research report, published in March 1984, was well received. The actual research methodology was in fact quite sound and the results that were reported in Part II were as reliable as most pieces of social investigation using self-completed questionnaire techniques. The full analysis moreover, supported the provisional figures published in the interim Report. It showed that 45% of schoolchildren in England and Wales had seen at least one violent video film.

The sample was a large one and was fully representative of social geography, geographical region and social class. By including some of the parents of the child respondents in the survey and asking them also to complete a questionnaire, this provided a valuable check upon the reliability of the data provided by the children. This was one of a number of techniques used to check the reliability of the children's data.

The problems of obtaining accurate information from children were fully recognised and were the subject of lengthy deliberations within the research team and the academic Working Party.

By prior arrangement with the school, each class participating in the survey had to follow a similar procedure. The children completed the questionnaires during class time and each child had to work alone without collusion or consultation with other children. Teachers were asked to explain the object of the survey to the children and to ensure that they did not think of it as an examination. They were asked to impress upon the children that it did not matter if they had seen none of the 113 films listed. The only essential was that they answered honestly. Teachers were also asked to ensure that the children could understand all the questions and different procedures were laid down for different age groups leaving the class teacher freedom to apply the rules according to the ability of their children. The teachers were also asked to lead a class discussion about the video films the children had seen after they had completed the questionnaires. This was to provide additional data relating to the children's viewing patterns and to act as a check upon the accuracy of the answers provided in the questionnaires.

As an additional reliability check many schools were visited by members of the research team who checked upon the procedure followed by the teachers and also carried out face-to-face interviews with the children. Many of these interviews were taped and the children were asked to describe the films they claimed to have seen in the answers they gave on their questionnaires. In this way additional checks were carried out on the accuracy and honesty of the answers provided in the completed questionnaires.

Much additional data was provided by the teachers themselves in their reports of class discussions. Further data was obtained from head teachers who often gave an overview of the situation in their school with age groups other than those included in the sample obtained from their school. Hence a dossier of anecdotal data was produced to go alongside the statistical data derived from the analysis of questionnaire returns.

Further checks upon the honesty and reliability of the children's answers were carried out when the questionnaires were coded. Any children who appeared to be over-claiming by saying that they had seen all or most of the 113 film titles listed were automatically discarded. Many of these children probably had seen one or more of the 'video nasties' but it was thought better to discard their questionnaires rather than to include data from unreliable respondents. A panel of teachers was used to adjudicate on doubtful questionnaires. The data provided by approximately 150 children was discarded through these reliability checks.

The academic Working Party and the research team were satisfied that the sampling techniques that they used together with the weighting procedures and reliability checks did produce trustworthy results. The whole Working Party put their names, and thereby their academic reputations, behind the veracity of the Report that was published on 7 March 1984. This Report received widespread favourable publicity in the media and was well received by the teaching profession. Most teachers, by this time, had become alerted to the situation existing in the country and were well aware of the fact that vast numbers of children of all ages were seeing video films that were rated for adult viewing many of which were of a particularly violent and horrific nature.

The empirical evidence of children's viewing patterns and the attitudes and opinions of their parents provided by the schools survey and published in the Report was generally acknowledged to have been influential in creating public awareness of the extent to which children were being exposed to violent and horrific scenes. In November 1983 when the Video Recordings Bill was given its second reading in the Commons very few MPs expected it to survive the session, but when the crucial votes were taken on 13 March and 6 July 1984 not one single MP voted against it.

The Bill did, however, have a difficult passage through the Lords where several Peers provided strong opposition. This was eventually overcome and the Bill returned to the Commons in time for its final reading and it duly reached the Statute Book receiving the Queen's Assent in July 1984. Provision was made for the Home Secretary to bring the Video Recordings Act into force through an Order in Council when the necessary preparations were completed.

Part III Research

The third part of the Enquiry continued beyond the passing of the Video Recordings Act. This concerned the effects upon children of their exposure to scenes of violence on video films. This research was designed to draw mainly upon data supplied by psychiatrists, paediatricians and educationalists. It is the results of this research that are the subject of this present book.

The research has been spread over a period of approximately 18 months and has not been tied to any Parliamentary timetable. Unlike the schools' survey, it has not been carried out against a background of a Parliamentary campaign or with the objective of providing evidence for proposed legislation. It is recognised that the social situation in Britain has changed considerably since the beginning of this research programme. Public opinion has run strongly against the uncontrolled availability of ultra-violent video films. That, together with a large number of prosecutions under the Obscene Publications Act 1959 has limited the availability to the public of the so-called 'video nasties'. There is therefore less chance today of children seeing ultra-violent video films than in 1983, although there is evidence that violent and obscene video films are being made available for home viewing through private video clubs. These operate on a mail order 'plain wrapper' basis and thus by-pass the restrictions placed upon the High Street video rental shops.

The research in this book into the effects upon children of their exposure to scenes of violence is presented out of a desire to increase our knowledge on an important social phenomenon that may be affecting the health of large numbers of children in Britain. Although it is largely non-statistical, the research nevertheless has an empirical basis. It has produced facts from a survey of professional men and women with considerable experience of working with children. Their experience and their professional opinions deserve to be closely studied.

Acknowledgments

I am indebted to all the members of the academic Working Party and others who read the draft of this chapter to ensure that it is factually correct.

4 The Findings of the National Viewers' Survey

Geoffrey K. Nelson

Who watches 'video nasties'? This was the central question that we set out to answer in the national survey of schoolchildren, the background to which has been outlined in the previous chapter.

The survey data was drawn from more than 4,500 school children of both sexes and aged between seven and sixteen years. The sample was fully representative in terms of geographical region, social geography and social class. The children were asked a variety of questions concerning their television and video viewing. This data was coded and analysed and the results were published in March 1984. The data is briefly summarised in this chapter.

For the purposes of this study we defined 'video nasties' as those feature films that contained scenes of such violence and sadism involving either human beings or animals that they would not be granted a certificate by the British Board of Film Censors (BBFC) for general release for public exhibition in Britain. Such films may be liable to prosecution by the Director of Public Prosecutions under the Obscene Publications Act 1959 Section 2.

We also took note of the adult films seen by children. These are films given an '18' or 'R18' rating by the British Board of Film Censors, as films that are considered unsuitable for public exhibition to persons below the age of 18. Some of these adult films are available on video cassette and may therefore be seen by children on home video sets.

Ownership of VCRs

A study published in 1983 by the International Institute of Communications revealed that 30.1% of homes in Britain with television sets also possessed a video cassette recorder (VCR). Our survey showed that 40.9% of children in our sample had a VCR in their homes. This would appear to indicate that households with children are more likely to have a VCR than those without children. Hence the results from our sample which was entirely composed of families with children of school age was 10% above the national average.

The ownership of VCRs was by no means evenly distributed throughout England and Wales but was much higher in the South East (including London) where it was 47.9% and lowest in Wales (27.0%). In general, ownership was high in the more urbanised regions (North West, 38.4%; East Midlands, 38.6%; North, 34.5%; Yorkshire, 34.8%; West Midlands, 33.1%) and lower in the more rural areas such as the South West (33.0%) and East Anglia (30.2%).

The differences between urban and rural regions were supported by the finding that irrespective of region, VCR ownership is higher in large towns than in the countryside.

Table 4.1   *Percentage of children who have a VCR at home by environment*

Environment	% who have a VCR at home
Village	27.7
Provincial town	37.4
Outer commuter	42.7
Suburb of city	45.7
Inner City	40.4
Total sample	40.9

The table shows that the highest rate of VCR ownership is to be found in the suburbs and outer commuter zones of large cities. These are areas that are predominantly middle class in social composition and relatively wealthy. However, the fact that VCR ownership is also high in inner city areas which are predominantly working class in composition indicates that class and wealth are not the only factors that influence ownership of VCRs. There is a need here for further research but it would appear that the most important factors are related to differing patterns of culture that affect the quality of life and to what may be broadly called urban-rural differences.

Most video viewers seem to rent their cassettes from what have become known as video clubs. These are video shops that act as a library for renting cassettes. Most of such shops operate a video club and only rent to members. Membership is a formality which often involves a fee that acts as a deposit to ensure the return of the cassette. However, in view of growing competition, many clubs now offer free membership. The survey showed that 79.4% of parents owning or renting VCRs were members of video clubs. In spite of the widespread ownership of VCRs many children watch video films outside their own homes, usually at the homes of friends or relatives. Nearly 80% of children said they had seen videos outside their own home. That is almost twice as many as have seen videos at home.

Videos on the DPP's List

In the summer of 1983 when this research was designed, a list of 32 violent horror films ('video nasties') available on video cassette was obtained from officers of Scotland Yard's Vice Squad and officers from the Obscene Publications Department of provincial forces. This list contained titles of video films that had been found obscene under the Obscene Publications Act 1959, or were at that time currently the subject of legal proceedings or being considered for prosecution by the Director of Public Prosecutions. We called this 'the DPP's list'.

A further list of the 100 most popular video films was obtained from video traders. The two lists were combined, randomised and put into the questionnaire that was given to the children in the National Viewers' Survey.

The children were not asked which video films they had seen or not seen, as this might have biased the results. Instead they were asked to score on a three point scale any that they had seen.

In the period between the summer of 1983 and January 1984 a further 21 video films had been added to the DPP's list. Three of these were already on the list of most popular videos and so were already included in our questionnaire.

Exposure to Videos on the DPP's List

Our study revealed that 45.5% of children in our sample had seen one or more of the video films on the DPP's list. If all 51 'obscene' videos on the DPP's list of January 1984 had been included in the questionnaire, it is likely that this figure would have been higher.

Table 4.2 *Percentage of children who have seen one or more videos on the DPP's list by age and sex*

		Age (Years) of children					
		7–8	9–10	11–12	13–14	15–16	All ages
Sex	*Boys*	34.7	54.0	48.1	58.1	59.6	50.7
	Girls	31.7	41.7	40.4	47.5	45.1	41.7
	Both	33.2	47.7	43.7	51.6	50.4	45.5

The table shows more boys than girls have seen 'video nasties' and the gap between the genders widens in the older age groups.

Children who have seen one or even two 'video nasties' may have done so accidentally, that is, without being aware of the type of film they were going to see, but if a child had seen four or more such films it was likely that they had deliberately chosen to view this type of video. It might be feasible to argue that such children had acquired a taste for this type of viewing, and the statistics for this group would consequently seem to indicate the number of children who might be assumed to have been more seriously committed to watching horrific and violent films.

It should be noted that the number of children who have seen four or more videos on the DPP's list is included in the number who have seen one or more, since a child who has seen four of these videos has obviously seen more than one of the films.

Table 4.3 *Percentage of children who have seen four or more videos on the DPP's list by age and sex*

		Age (Years) of children					
		7–8	9–10	11–12	13–14	15–16	All ages
Sex	*Boys*	16.2	29.6	23.9	34.1	30.6	26.9
	Girls	11.6	19.8	16.1	22.0	18.6	18.1
	Both	13.8	24.6	19.3	26.7	22.9	21.8

The table above shows that 21.8% of children between the ages of 7 and 16 have seen four or more videos on the DPP's list. Again we find that boys are more likely than girls to have seen four or more of these films. It is also clear that older children are more likely to have seen this type of film than younger children.

The table on the next page shows that the regular watching of these video films is higher in inner city areas and commuter districts and lower in villages and suburbs.

Table 4.4 *Percentage of children who have seen none, one or more, four or more videos on the DPP's list by environment*

		Environment					
		Village	Provincial town	Outer commuter	Suburb of city	Inner city	Total sample
No. of DPP Videos Seen	0	71.0	52.6	44.2	59.4	45.5	54.5
	1+	29.0	47.4	55.8	40.6	54.5	45.5
	4+	12.2	25.6	26.4	16.4	29.8	21.8

In the inner city and commuter areas over 50% of children have seen at least one 'video nasty' and over 25% have seen four or more. In villages, however, 71% have *never* seen this type of video. The factors relating to these variations in viewing patterns are unknown and need further study.

Regional Viewing Patterns

There are also regional differences that remain unexplained. For example, the proportion of regular viewers of films on the DPP's list is highest in the North and North West regions and lowest in East Anglia and Wales. An anomaly is revealed in the areas of the South East which in spite of having the highest rate of VCR ownership has a relatively low proportion of regular viewers of videos on the DPP's list.

Table 4.5 *Percentage of children who have seen none, one or more, four or more videos on the DPP's list by region*

		Region									
		North	Yorks	E. Mids	E. Anglia	S. East	S. West	W. Mids	N. West	Wales	Total sample
No. of DPP Video Films Seen	0	42.6	54.6	52.0	68.5	56.0	64.0	53.8	42.4	73.8	54.5
	1+	57.4	45.4	48.0	31.5	44.0	36.0	46.2	57.6	26.2	45.5
	4+	34.1	22.7	27.5	10.5	19.2	18.7	20.0	30.6	9.8	21.8

Regional differences are difficult to explain because most of the regions lack a clear social homogeneity. The two regions with the lowest viewing rate are largely rural but both contain large urban centres (Cardiff and Swansea in Wales; Norwich and Ipswich in East Anglia). The North West, which has the highest figures for children seeing videos on the DPP's list, is heavily urbanised. The area includes Greater Manchester, Merseyside and the urbanised areas of South Lancashire.

The North includes not only the industrialised areas of the North East but also the rural areas of Cumbria. The West Midlands includes not only the Birmingham conurbation but the rural areas of Hereford, Worcestershire and Shropshire.

Regional differences may be related to the cultural traditions of the regions, though some of the Registrar General's regions have little historical or cultural unity and have been designated as such for administrative convenience.

Regional patterns of viewing may also be related to factors such as unemployment that have not been included in the study.

Many children have seen a 'video nasty' at the home of a friend or relative. Indeed, children who have a VCR at home but also watch videos outside the home are most likely to have been exposed to this type of film. Our study shows that 64.9% of children in this category have seen at least one 'video nasty' and 37.3% have seen four or more. Some children also will have seen such films at youth clubs, schools and other places outside the home.

We received reports to indicate that children pool their pocket money to rent video films including 'video nasties' and meet after school hours to watch them in one another's homes, perhaps in a home where both parents are at work. One youth club leader reporting on such a 'neighbourhood' group, stated that the children 'take it in turns to choose the films and compete with each other as to who can rent the nastiest "nasty" '.

Obscene Video Films

We now turn to an examination of children's views on the 'video nasties' they had seen. In the following table we list the top ten violent horror films. These are the films from the DPP's list which have been seen by the greatest numbers of children.

Table 4.6   *Percentage of children who have seen the 'Top Ten' most seen video films drawn from the DPP's list*

Title	%
The Evil Dead	18.4
Zombie Flesh-Eaters	17.8
The Living Dead	15.9
The Bogey Man	15.8
The Burning	12.1
I Spit on Your Grave	11.7
Death Trap	11.6
Zombie Creeping Flesh	11.3
Zombie Terror	10.1
Driller Killer	9.7

These video cassettes have been widely available throughout England and Wales. However, many readers may have little idea of the content of these films, so a synopsis has been included in Appendix 3.

The film *The Evil Dead* which has been seen most frequently by children was given a British Board of Film Censors certificate and shown in British cinemas before being prosecuted by the DPP. Despite being given an '18' rating it should not have been seen by children in our sample. Even if some older children had seen it illegally in the cinema, the great majority must have seen it on video.

In addition to being checked the most times in the list of 113 video titles we presented to the children, the title *The Evil Dead* was written out by hand by far the most number of times of all the films on the DPP's list in the children's questionnaire under their favourite films and their most remembered video titles. Although we have received numerous accounts of children being disturbed by this film, it is not possible to quantify these or to give any accurate figures of how many children are involved, or what percentage of those who have seen it have been disturbed. We therefore quote below one such documented case without any claim as to its representativeness.

An 11-year-old boy in the Harrow/North London area was invited to a birthday party and along with a group of other 11-year-olds was shown *The Evil Dead*. The host parents said afterwards they were not aware of the content of the film and they did not remain in the room to watch it with the children. They had left it to an older teenage boy to rent an appropriate film for the children. The child went home in a disturbed state of mind and described to his parents some of what he had seen. His father went and remonstrated with the other child's parents. That night, for the first time since infancy, the boy wetted the bed. The following night he awoke the whole household screaming. He was disturbed for several more nights saying that he could not get out of his mind the high pitched chanting of the possessed woman in the film, 'We're going to get you! We're going to get you!'

The five *'favourite'* 'video nasty' titles written by hand by the children in their questionnaires were: *The Evil Dead, The Burning, Zombie Flesh-Eaters, I Spit on your Grave* and *The Living Dead.*

Children were also asked to write out their *'most remembered'* video film titles. These were not necessarily their favourites, as was judged from some of their comments. The five titles on the DPP's list recorded the most number of times were: *The Evil Dead, The Burning, Zombie Flesh-Eaters, The Living Dead* and *Driller Killer.*

Adult Films

Although this study was designed to investigate the viewing patterns of children in relation to 'video nasties' we also included in our questionnaire a number of adult or '18' rated films in the list given to the children. The content of these films is usually either violence, horror, occult, sex or a combination of these. These films will have been given a certificate for showing only to adults over the age of 18. Such films are also available on video cassette and these may be seen by children under 17. We found that 57.3% of children aged 7 to 16 had seen at least one, and 29.5% had seen four or more of this type of film, presumably at home, though some older children might have illegally obtained admission to a cinema showing one of these films. One of the adult films included in our list had been shown on late night television.

The children were asked to list their 'favourite' and 'most remembered' films. The following '18' rated films were mentioned most frequently:

Poltergeist
An American Werewolf in London
Friday the 13th
Mad Max
The Thing
One Flew over the Cuckoo's Nest
Texas Chain Saw Massacre
Private Lessons
The Shining

Over the past 10 years the degree of explicit sex and violence in '18' (X) rated films has grown considerably. In 1974 *Cinema TV Today* described the film *The Nun and the Devil* as containing 'a steaming brew of sadomasochistic delights'. Of *Sex without Love*, it said 'the film is a conglomeration of copulations, rapes and killings . . .'. In 1976 the British Film Institute's monthly film bulletin describing a scene in *Death Weekend* said '. . . Runt the smallest of the gang is given permission by Rep to rape Di in her bedroom, but she cuts his throat with a sliver of broken glass and escapes from the house . . .'. *Screen International* rated it as 'Primarily for lovers of all-out violence laced with sex'.

The 'R18' film category is fairly new and was only introduced in 1980. These films are restricted for showing only on premises specifically licensed to show them. In general they contain more violence and explicit sex than the '18' rated films. It may be said that where the level of sexual explicity reaches a certain level the film may be considered unsuitable for public exhibition but may still be seen in restricted situations. 'R18' films may, however, be available on video cassette and thus seen by children. Some films initially given an 'R18' rating by the BBFC have subsequently been found to be obscene under the Obscene Publications Act 1959, so that the situation with regard to the 'R18' rating is unclear. Further confusion arises from the fact that the police are prosecuting some video films that they consider to be 'R18' material which have not been certified as such by the BBFC.

The problem arises from the lack of a clear definition of obscenity. Some police officers take the view that the standards for judging what constitutes pornography have changed rapidly over the past few years. They say that what used to be called 'hard porn' is now being called 'soft porn'. They also say that the whole situation has become ridiculous in that in film sequences depicting explicit human intercourse, a policeman now has to use a ruler to measure to the nearest millimetre whether there is actual contact between the sex organs as a means of distinguishing between 'hard' and 'soft' porn.

Our survey reveals that children of all ages throughout England and Wales are seeing videos of all types. It is, moreover, reasonable to assume that for many children films of this type provide their first introduction to human sexual behaviour.

Parents' Study

A total of 2,557 parents completed questionnaires for the survey in a nationally representative sample. The main aim of the study was to discover the attitudes of parents towards their children's actual or possible exposure to scenes of horrific violence on video films. In the first place parents were asked: 'What would you do if you found out that your child(ren) had been watching videos at a friend's house, and you thought that these videos were unsuitable?' They were asked to indicate which of a number of forms of action they would take. The results are shown in Table 4.7 on the next page.

Table 4.7   *Percentage of parents choosing each action*

Actions	%
Report the incident to the police	1.8
Go and see the parents	47.1
Stop your child from visiting the house	39.6
Be very angry at the incident but decide not to do anything	3.1
Contact your MP	0.4
There would be no need to do anything	1.8
Discuss the incident with your child	69.4

The findings strongly suggest a wide acceptance of two assumptions: that there is a problem of supervision and control, and that this is essentially a problem experienced within the family which has to be handled with the resources available to the family itself. It is interesting to note that 69% said they would discuss the incident with the child. Only 1.8% said: 'There would be no need to do anything about it'.

The vast majority of parents showed a high level of 'responsible protectiveness' towards their children. Of course 'unsuitable' videos introduced uncertainty into the situation for some parents might consider 'video nasties' to be suitable viewing for their children. In order to discover the type of programmes which parents would consider unsuitable for children, we asked parents to indicate at what age they would allow their children to view certain specified television programmes. The following Tables (4.8–4.10) give the key findings.

Table 4.8 *Percentage of parents allowing their child(ren) to watch television programmes containing scenes of violence only when they are over certain ages*

		Age (Years) of children					
		Any age	Over 5	Over 10	Over 12	Over 15	Over 18
TV Programmes	Minder	9.9	14.2	27.5	21.4	6.1	1.6
	Hill Street Blues	8.8	6.7	16.4	19.6	13.8	3.4
	War news	17.8	17.1	22.7	17.2	5.9	1.6
	Professionals	10.2	17.5	28.9	19.6	5.9	1.6
	The Sweeney	9.0	11.1	23.0	22.0	9.9	2.2

Table 4.9 *Percentage of parents allowing their child(ren) to watch television programmes containing sexual innuendo only when they are over certain ages*

		Age (Years) of children					
		Any age	Over 5	Over 10	Over 12	Over 15	Over 18
TV Programmes	Benny Hill	14.1	22.3	23.6	14.3	5.9	3.8
	Carry On films	26.5	32.1	20.7	7.9	2.7	1.4

Table 4.10   *Percentage of parents allowing their child(ren) to watch television programmes only when they are over certain ages*

		Age (Years) of children					
		Any age	Over 5	Over 10	Over 12	Over 15	Over 18
TV Programmes	Tom & Jerry	93.7	4.4	0.2	0.2	0.0	0.0
	Cagney & Lacey	11.8	14.7	25.7	18.9	4.9	1.4
	Play For Today	10.3	6.1	17.6	23.2	12.6	1.9
	Kenny Everett	12.7	24.8	24.2	15.7	5.6	3.1
	Dallas	18.3	21.2	23.1	13.1	3.8	1.4
	Grange Hill	31.4	39.5	17.1	3.5	0.7	0.7
	Dukes Of Hazzard	39.3	39.4	12.9	2.5	0.2	0.0

None of these programmes are in any way to be considered as equivalent to 'video nasties' but the parents' responses indicate their attitude towards children's viewing. Most parents put few restrictions on the viewing of children over the age of 12. It is also interesting to note that news programmes which may contain much explicit violence are the subject of restrictions by few parents, though the view has been expressed that viewing factual violence may be more harmful than viewing fictional violence.

If parents are so concerned about their children's viewing habits how is it that a large number of children under the age of 12 have seen one or more video films depicting violence? This is not a question that can be directly answered from the data collected, but there are two probable contributing factors. Parents may not be aware of the nature of the video films that their children are watching, which might seem to indicate a lack of supervision in the home. On the other hand many children have seen such videos outside the home and their parents might not be aware of the type of film they are seeing in friends' houses.

Parents were asked to respond to expressions of opinions about children's television and the issue of responsibility and their views are summarised in the next two tables. The opinions they were asked to respond to were as follows:

1 Left to themselves children will only watch what is good for them.
2 It doesn't matter what children watch.
3 Any film which is considered not to be obscene should be available to adults from their video library.
4 Only films which have been passed by the British Board of Film Censors for public exhibition should be available in video libraries.
5 Society has a duty to protect children from uncensored video films.
6 Parents should have the final responsibility as to what their children should, or should not, watch.
7 There are too many children's programmes on television.
8 There should be a separate channel for children's television.
9 Children watch too much television.
10 Parents allow their children to watch too much television.

NB   The statements in the above list are not in the same order as they were in the questionnaire.

Table 4.11   *Percentage of parents who agree or disagree with the statements on children's television*

Opinion Number	Agree Strongly	Agree	Neither Agree Nor Disagree	Disagree	Disagree Strongly
7	1.3	3.4	28.7	58.3	7.0
8	8.8	28.9	16.8	38.6	5.4
9	13.3	45.6	22.4	16.0	0.9
10	10.0	44.3	22.4	17.7	2.3

It is interesting to note that a majority of parents believe that children watch too much television and that 'parents allow their children to watch too much television'.

From the point of view of our survey the findings in Table 4.12 on the next page are more significant.

Table 4.12 *Percentage of parents who agree or disagree with the statements on protection of children*

Opinion Number	Agree Strongly	Agree	Neither Agree Nor Disagree	Disagree	Disagree Strongly
1	1.7	10.8	6.6	52.8	26.3
2	0.8	2.4	3.3	43.8	47.7
3	7.8	60.4	16.5	8.9	2.3
4	15.2	44.0	13.6	21.0	3.9
5	49.9	40.3	3.6	2.8	1.0
6	38.5	51.2	3.4	4.3	0.5

The view expressed in the first two statements implying that parents should not be concerned about their children's viewing either because children are able to choose for themselves or because it doesn't matter what they watch, was rejected by over 75% of all parents.

Twelve per cent of parents thought that their children could be trusted to choose for themselves. It may be that these are the parents of older children or those who have a greater confidence in their own children's ability to discern what is good for them as a result of the home environment training and upbringing.

The majority of respondents (68.2%) believed that 'any film which is considered not to be obscene should be available to adults from their video library', a view which indicated that most people respect the right of free choice of adult individuals in this country. However, almost 60% of parents believed that *only* those films which had been passed by the British Board of Film Censors should be available for public viewing.

The final two statements regarding the responsibility of society and parents for children might seem at first sight to be contradictory as most parents agreed with both. On closer examination these statements are not contradictory but complementary. Most people seem to take the view that while most parents have ultimate responsibility for their children, they need the support of society in order to carry out their duties. Children need to be protected not only within the home where parents may be presumed to exercise control but also outside the home where they may be exposed to influences over which parents can exercise little direct control. Furthermore it must be recognised that some parents do not accept their responsibilities while others may not be able to exercise the control necessary and in these cases it becomes the responsibility of the state (society) to take over their responsibilities and exercise control.

Matched Sample Analysis

A 20% random sample of the total population of the National Viewers' Survey was selected for an in-depth study of the relationship between children's and parents' responses. The sample was matched with the national social class structure and was representative of geographical area.

We found that the age of parents did not appear to be a significant factor in the number of films on the DPP's list seen by children. However, social class did appear to be a significant factor.

The social class of the families was assessed using the six-point Registrar General's scale of Social Class by occupation, i.e.

Social Class 1 – high professional and executive.
Social Class 2 – professional and high administrative.
Social Class 3N – non-manual clerical grades.
Social Class 3M – skilled manual.
Social Class 4 – semi-skilled manual.
Social Class 5 – unskilled manual.

The findings are given in Tables 4.13–4.15.

Table 4.13 *Percentage of children who have a VCR at home by social class*

	Social class						
	1	2	3N	3M	4	5	Total sample
VCR at home	38.7	37.0	44.7	50.0	41.7	27.8	39.5

Table 4.14   *Percentage of children who have seen none, one or more, four or more videos on the DPP's list by social class*

		Social class						
		1	2	3N	3M	4	5	Total sample
No. of DPP Videos Seen	0	61.3	63.0	51.8	52.8	46.3	38.9	53.8
	1+	38.7	37.0	48.2	47.2	53.7	61.1	46.2
	4+	22.6	13.0	20.0	25.5	25.0	27.8	20.9

Table 4.15   *Percentage of children who have seen none, one or more, four or more '18' videos by social class*

		Social class						
		1	2	3N	3M	4	5	Total sample
No. of '18' Video Films Seen	0	51.6	50.0	41.2	38.7	33.3	22.2	39.6
	1+	48.4	50.0	58.8	61.3	66.7	77.8	60.4
	4+	25.8	27.2	29.4	34.0	37.0	41.7	29.9

It is clear from Table 4.14 that the lower the social class the more likely it is that children will have seen one or more, and four or more videos on the DPP's list though there is a slight increase in class 1 (the highest social class). The situation with regard to the viewing of '18' rated films is similar. Our data does not provide an explanation for this relationship between class and viewing and further research needs to be carried out.

It was found that the children of parents with a more 'authoritarian' attitude were less likely to have seen 'video nasties' than were the children of 'lenient' parents. The children of parents who took the view that 'there was no need to do anything' when their children had seen an unsuitable video at a friend's house were much more likely to have seen four or more 'nasties' than were the children of parents who gave any other response. By contrast 81% of the children whose parents said they would report the incident to the police had never seen a 'nasty'.

It would seem that the attitude of parents is a major factor in determining children's viewing habits. In particular it is related to parental attitudes towards authority within the family.

However, it is clear that some children of authoritarian and 'protective' parents do see violent horror films. It would seem therefore that some such parents are unable for various reasons to enforce their attitudes.

Summary

1 Forty-five per cent of the children aged 7 to 16 years in the sample had seen one or more of the violent horrific video films, legally found to be obscene in Britain and known as the 'video nasties'. By the age of 8, one-third of all the children in the sample had seen a 'video nasty'.

2 More boys than girls watch the violent horrific video films. 50.7% of boys and 41.7% of girls have seen one or more.

3 Fifty-seven per cent of children aged 7 to 16 years in the sample had seen at least one '18' rated film, ie films intended for adult viewing. By the age of 10, half of all the children in our sample had seen an '18' rated adult film.

4 The children's favourite '18' rated adult films are horror, occult or pornographic. For many of the children the obscene and adult rated films may represent their introduction to human sexual activity through scenes of explicit violence, rape and sexual deviance.

5 Sixty per cent of children aged 7 to 16 years in the sample who watch video films at a friend's or relative's house had seen a 'video nasty' and 34% of them had seen four or more.

6 Half of all the children in the sample (50.7%) aged 7 to 16 years who had a VCR in their home had seen one or more of the 'video nasties'.

7 Children in urban areas are more likely to see violent horrific video films than those in rural areas. Cultural as well as social class variables appear to be determinants in children's viewing patterns.

8 The attitude of parents appears to be a major determinant of children's viewing patterns. The children of 'lenient' parents in our survey had seen significantly more 'video nasties' than those of 'protective' parents.

9 Most parents in the survey were concerned to protect their children from seeing what they considered to be unsuitable video films. The large majority reported that they wished to exercise some control over their children's viewing.

10 In addition to exercising their own control, 90% of parents in the sample believed that society has a duty to help them protect their children from seeing uncensored video films.

11 Many parents appear to be unaware that their children are seeing 'video nasties' or '18' rated films.

12 It is the inescapable conclusion of this survey that any video film available for home viewing will be seen by a significant number of children of all ages.

Acknowledgments

I would like to thank all the schools who participated in the National Viewers' Survey and every child, parent and teacher who completed a questionnaire.

I would also like to express my gratitude to all the members of the Working Party and Research Team who were involved in this part of the Enquiry, in particular Howard Davis, Robert Holman and Clifford Hill.

National Viewers' Survey Questionnaires

The following is a condensed version of the questionnaires put to the children and to the parents.

Children's Questionnaire

Please ask your teacher to help you answer anything you do not understand.
Please put a circle around the number which is next to your answer.

SECTION ONE

1   Are you a boy?
    Are you a girl?

2   How old are you?
    5 to 6 years old
    7 to 8 years old
    9 to 10 years old
    11 to 12 years old
    13 to 14 years old
    15 to 16 years old
    17 to 18 years old

3   Which comics or magazines do you read?

4   What are the titles of your favourite 3 books?

5   What are the names of your favourite 3 pop groups?

6   Name the titles of your favourite 3 films

    If you saw the film in the CINEMA put a circle around C.
    If you saw the film on TV (BBC or ITV/Channel 4) put a circle around TV.
    If you saw the film on VIDEO put a circle around V.
    If you saw the film on TV and VIDEO for example then circle both.

7   Name your favourite 3 TV programmes (BBC or ITV/Channel 4).

8   Name your favourite 3 TV Stars.

9   Do you have a home computer?

10   Do you have a video recorder at home?

11   Name your favourite 3 video games.

12   Does your family belong to a video club?

13   Have you ever been to a friend's or relative's house to watch video films?

14   Can you remember titles of any videos you have seen?
      If yes, which ones can you remember most?

SECTION TWO

Below is a list of popular video films.

If you have seen any of these films ON VIDEO put a circle around one of the numbers.
If you thought it was GREAT put a circle around 1.
If you thought it was JUST ALRIGHT [*sic*] put a circle around 2.
If you thought it was AWFUL put a circle around 3.

If you have NOT seen a film on video DO NOT CIRCLE ANY OF THE NUMBERS but go on to the next film in the list.

Superman II
Every Which Way But Loose
FIST
Dogs of War
Airplane
Absurd
Fort Apache – The Bronx
Herbie Rides Again
Private Lessons
Rocky
Blood Feast
Escape From New York
Stripes
Amityville II – The Possession
Bogie Man
Chariots of Fire
Jabberwocky
Conquest of the Earth
For your Eyes Only
Cannibal Apocalypse
Midnight Express
Smokie and the Bandit
Snuff
Mad Max

Cannibal Ferox
Creepshow
Grease
Contamination
Funhouse
Stir Crazy
Death Trap
ET
Cannibal Man
Gone in 60 seconds
The Shining
The Love Bug
Possession
The French Lieutenant's Woman
Gallipoli
The Burning
Buck Rogers in the 25th Century
Zombie Terror
Wolfen
Fanny Hill
Zombie Flesh Eaters
Octopussy
The Secret of Nimh
The Living Dead

An American Werewolf in London
Dead and Buried
Star Wars
SS Experiment Camp
Bronx Warriors
The Beast in Heat
Victor/Victoria
Rocky II
Cannibal Holocaust
The Long Riders
Friday the 13th Part 2
Cat People
Pranks
Watership Down
Foul Play
The Last House on the Left
The Slayer
Jaws 2
Poltergeist
Zombie Creeping Flesh
Piranha
Bedknobs and Broomsticks
Confessions of a Driving Instructor
The Cannonball Run
Driller Killer
Flash Gordon
Don't Go In The House
Kramer vs Kramer
Mardi Gras Massacre
Gregory's Girl
Conan the Barbarian
Sharkey's Machine
Nightmares in a Damaged Brain

Superman
Scrubbers
The Champ
I Spit on Your Grave
Battle Star Galactica
One Flew Over the Cuckoo's Nest
Q – The Winged Serpent
Bloody Man
Death Wish II
The Border
The Thing
Return of The Jedi
Don't Go in the Woods Alone
Sorceress
Caligula
Rocky II
Night of the Demon
First Blood
Annie
The Evil Dead
Mad Max II
Texas Chain Saw Massacre
Faces of Death
The World's Greatest Athlete
The Sentinel
House on the Edge of the Park
Vigilante
Evil Speak
Life of Brian
Cannibal Terror
Any Which Way You Can
The Howling

Parents' Questionnaire

Please put a circle around the number(s)
which corresponds to your answer.

1 What is/are your occupation(s)?

2 Are you: an owner occupier
            in rented accommodation

3 Which Sunday papers did you read
   last Sunday?
   Sunday Times
   Mail on Sunday
   Sunday People
   Sunday Mirror

The Observer
Sunday Express
Sunday Telegraph
News of the World
Any other
None

4 Which daily papers did you read
   this week? (Ring more than one if
   you read more than one.)
   The Guardian
   Daily Mirror
   Daily Mail

Daily Star
Daily Express
The Sun
The Times
The Daily Telegraph
Morning Star
Financial Times
Others
None

5 Do you have a video recorder in your home?

6a Can you remember any books you read to your child?

6b If yes, could you please tell us the last two books?

7a Have you ever taken your child to the cinema?

7b If yes, what was the name of the last film you took your child to see?

8 What would you do if you found out that your child(ren) had been watching videos at a friend's house, and you thought that those videos were unsuitable. Please circle the appropriate number(s).

Report the incident to the Police
Go and see the parents
Stop your child from visiting the house
Be very angry at the incident, but decide not to do anything
Contact your MP
There would be no need to do anything
Discuss the incident with your child

9 At what age do/did you allow your child(ren) to watch the following BBC/ITV series in your home? Please put a tick in the appropriate column on the right.

Tom and Jerry   Cagney and
Benny Hill   Lacey
  Show   Hill Street
Minder   Blues

News reel film   Dallas
  of war/   The Sweeney
  terrorist   Grange Hill
  activity   Dukes of
Play for Today   Hazzard
Professionals   Carry On films
Kenny Everett
  Show

10 Are you:
Male
Female

11 Are you aged:

21–25	46–50
26–30	51–55
31–35	56–60
36–40	61–65
41–45	66 or over

Here are some things which people have said about children and television.
Please give your opinion by ticking in the appropriate column.

1 There are too many children's programmes on TV.
2 There should be a separate channel for children's television.
3 Left to themselves children will only watch what is good for them.
4 Any film which is considered not to be obscene should be available to adults from their video library.
5 It doesn't matter what children watch.
6 Only films which have been passed by the British Board of Film Censors for public exhibition should be available in video libraries.
7 Children watch too much TV.
8 Society has a duty to protect children from uncensored video films.
9 Parents should have the final responsibility as to what their children should, or should not, watch.
10 Parents allow their children to watch too much TV.

5 NSPCC Survey

Alison Hill

This section of the research was designed to examine the viewing patterns and attitudes of parents and children in families with problems involving children, and to compare these findings with the results of a concurrent, but more general, survey into viewing patterns and attitudes of families of schoolchildren in England and Wales. The results of this general survey of children's viewing patterns and parental attitudes are taken from the National Viewers' Survey which is reported in Chapter 4 of this book. The sample of 'underprivileged' families is taken from those families visited by officers of the National Society for the Prevention of Cruelty to Children (NSPCC). This survey was carried out in December 1983 and January 1984.

The NSPCC is committed to providing immediate help for children in need. Invariably this means working with the whole family, helping them to overcome problems and difficulties. In about a third of the cases which come to the Society the parents themselves have asked for help and advice. The problems affecting these families range from debt and poor housing, through difficulties coping with their children's behaviour to the physical and sexual abuse of the children.

The main problem disturbing the families who contributed to this research on viewing patterns was recorded by the officers of the NSPCC. Behavioural problems in the child or children and housing and/or financial problems were the most frequently recorded difficulties. Nearly 20% of the families were having problems with their children's behaviour and 18% had housing and/or financial problems. In 15% of the families neglect was the main problem. Five per cent of the cases involved the physical abuse of the child or children and a further 12% were assessed by the officers to be at risk of physical abuse. The remainder of the families were recorded as having a variety of other problems.

The design used was similar to that used in the National Viewers' Survey. It was based on self-completion questionnaires, for parents and for children, which were taken to the families by the NSPCC officers when they visited. The officers were instructed to ask the parents of school-age children to complete a questionnaire during their next visit to that family. Questionnaires were also to be completed by any children aged between 7 and 16 years who were at home at the time of the visit. Stamped addressed envelopes and children's questionnaires were left by the officer for each school-age child who was not at home during the visit, and for those parents who preferred to fill in the questionnaire privately.

Seven hundred and sixty-five parents' questionnaires and 722 children's questionnaires were completed.

Who are the Families?

The children's questionnaires were completed by children of both sexes between the ages of 7 and 16. Fifty-two per cent of the children were boys. The 7- to 8-year-olds formed the largest age group (28%) with decreasing numbers of children in the older age groups (10% of children were aged 15 to 16 years).

The parents' questionnaires were completed by one or both parents. Fifty-eight per cent were completed by the mother, 10% by the father and 32% of the questionnaires were completed by the mother and the father together. The parents ranged in age from 'under 21' years (6.3%) to '66 and over' (0.1%). The majority of the parents were aged between 21 and 25 years (34.1%) and 26 and 30 years (34.8%).

The parents all had children under 16 years-old and 99% had children under 5 years. Thirty-eight per cent of the parents had children aged 5 to 6 while decreasing numbers of the parents in this sample had children in the older age groups. (Thirty-one per cent of the parents had children aged 7 to 8; 26% had children aged 9 to 10; 24% had children aged 11 to 12; 19% had children aged 13 to 14; and 12% had children aged 15 to 16 years.) The majority of parents had either one, two or three children, although almost 20% of the parents had four or more children under 16 years.

The sample of families was taken from all areas of England and Wales. The nine regions used were the same regions as those used in the regular National Census by the Registrar General and also in the National Viewers' Survey. The following are the nine regions used with the percentage of families from that region in brackets: North (13.7%); Yorkshire (6.9%); East Midlands (5.9%); East Anglia (1.3%); South East (24.3%); South West (11.0%); West Midlands (9.3%); North West (19.3%); Wales (7.3%). The sample was made up of families from each of the regions, although East Anglia and the East Midlands were under-represented while the South East (including London) and the North West (including Liverpool and Manchester) were over-represented. This uneven distribution may be due to the fact that there are more families referred to the NSPCC in the densely populated city areas than in the sparsely populated East of England.

The families were taken from a number of areas with different environments. The majority of the families (64%) lived in a suburban area while 18% lived in a rural area and 14% lived in the inner city.

The social class of the families was assessed using the six-point Registrar General's scale of Social Class by occupation, i.e.

Social Class 1 – high professional and executive.
Social Class 2 – professional and high administrative.
Social Class 3N – non-manual clerical grades.
Social Class 3M – skilled manual.
Social Class 4 – sem-skilled manual.
Social Class 5 – unskilled manual.

It was not possible to determine the social class of all the families since many parents were unemployed or single-parent housewives. In fact, 35% did not state their occupation.

However, of those families for whom a social class could be determined, the vast majority belonged to Social Class 5 (43%) or Social Class 4 (27%). Only one family could be classified as belonging to Social Class 1 and 8 families in Social Class 2. This sample is therefore very unevenly distributed in terms of social class and probably reflects the general social class structure of the families helped by the NSPCC.

Almost 85% of the families in this sample live in rented accommodation. This is much higher than in the general population and is no doubt linked to the social class of the sample.

Ownership and Viewing Patterns

Ninety-seven per cent of the families in this sample have a television. This is comparable with the national figures for television ownership. Twenty-two per cent of the families in this sample own or rent a video cassette recorder (VCR). This is much lower than either the national figure for 1983 (30%) or the figure obtained through the National Viewers' Survey (41%). The number of families who own or rent a VCR in the National Viewers' Survey is considerably higher than the national average and was explained by the hypothesis that VCRs are bought or hired mainly to entertain children, or for the use of young parents who must stay at home because of the demands of child rearing. The VCR therefore quite naturally becomes a *family* interest. This sample of underprivileged families seen by the NSPCC officers is generally of a lower socio-economic status than the general population and although they are families, the lower percentage of VCR ownership could be explained by economic factors.

A table showing the distribution of VCRs according to the age and sex of the child is given below.

Table 5.1 *Percentage of children who have a VCR at home by age and sex*

		Age (Years) of children					
		7–8	9–10	11–12	13–14	15–16	All ages
Sex	*Boys*	24.1	23.9	15.9	23.0	31.3	22.7
	Girls	17.4	23.4	18.5	20.6	23.3	20.3
	Both	20.9	23.7	17.9	22.2	26.7	21.7

There does not seem to be much of a pattern in ownership of VCRs by age and sex. VCRs seem to be most commonly found in the homes of 15- to 16-year-old boys, and are least common where there are 11- to 12-year-old boys. On the whole there appear to be more VCRs in the homes of boys than girls.

The figure below shows in graphical form the difference between the two samples in the percentage of children who have a VCR at home according to the age and sex of the children. Clearly, a much higher percentage of children in the National Viewers' Survey have a VCR at home than children in the NSPCC sample.

Fig. 5.1 *Percentage of children in each sample who have a VCR at home by age and sex.*

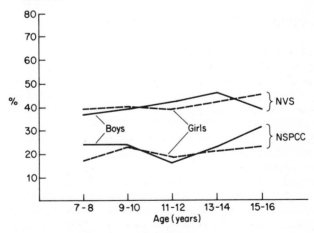

The results of the National Viewers' Survey showed that a very high percentage of schoolchildren watch videos at a friend's or relative's house (79.7%). The following table shows the percentage of schoolchildren in this

sample who have seen a video film at a friend's or relative's house according
to the age and sex of the child.

Table 5.2   *Percentage of children who have watched video films at a friend's or
relative's house by age and sex*

		Age (Years) of children					
		7–8	9–10	11–12	13–14	15–16	All ages
Sex	*Boys*	65.7	73.9	69.5	86.9	87.5	73.9
	Girls	53.3	64.9	75.4	82.5	83.7	69.4
	Both	59.7	69.8	70.9	84.1	85.3	71.3

The overall percentage of children in this sample who have seen video films at
friends' houses is, as expected, very high. Over 70% of children have been to
a friend's house to watch a video, and although this percentage is slightly
lower than the comparable figure in the general survey (79.7%), the age and
sex differences are much more marked in the underprivileged sample. The
table above shows that *many more boys than girls* watch videos at friends'
houses and this is true throughout the age groups (apart from 11- to
12-year-olds, where more girls apparently visit friends' houses to watch
videos than do boys. This may reflect a more general pattern of visiting in
that age group and not be specifically related to video watching.). In the general survey there was virtually no overall difference between the sexes, with
the younger boys watching more videos at a friend's house than girls, while
the older girls watched more videos at a friend's house than the same age boys.

The age differences are also much more marked in the underprivileged
sample with less than 60% of 7- to 8-year-olds watching videos at a friend's
while over 85% of 15- to 16-year-olds do. These age differences cannot be
seen so strikingly in the general survey with 70% of 7- to 8-year-olds seeing
videos at a friend's or relative's house. Could it be that the underprivileged
sample are more protective of their young children? Or do they have fewer
friends with VCRs at home because the density of video ownership in
economically deprived areas is lower?

It is interesting to note that in the general survey the number of children
who have seen video films outside their own home is almost twice as many as
those who have seen videos within their own home. However, in this sample
only 20% have VCRs at home while over 70% of children have seen videos at
a friend's house. That is three and a half times the number who have seen
videos in their own home.

The table below shows the percentage of parents who have watched a video at a friend's or relative's house, broken down by the age and sex of the parents.

Table 5.3   *Percentage of parents who have watched video films at a friend's or relative's house by age and sex*

		Age (Years)								
		Under 21	21–25	26–30	31–35	36–40	41–45	46–50	Over 50	All ages
Sex	*Male*	87.5	79.4	74.0	71.6	51.0	65.0	56.3	18.8	67.1
	Female	87.5	75.8	74.1	58.2	56.1	31.0	33.0	28.6	67.3
	Total	87.5	76.6	74.1	62.8	53.8	44.9	46.4	21.7	67.2

Sixty-seven per cent of parents in this sample have watched a video film at a friend's or relative's house. This shows that *watching videos is almost as popular a pastime with the adults as it is with the children in this sample.*

The table above also shows that there is no overall sex difference in the percentage of parents who have watched a video film at a friend's house. However, there is a very striking age difference in that many more young parents watch videos at friends' houses than do the older parents.

The parents in this sample were also asked whether their children had ever watched a video film at a friend's or relative's house. Only 57% of the parents said that their children had seen a video at a friend's house. Seventy-one per cent of the children said that they had. This discrepancy could be due to overclaiming by the children or more possibly it could be due to the parents simply not knowing what their children do in their leisure time.

What do They Watch?

A list of 113 video film titles was given in both the children's and the parents' questionnaires. The respondents were asked to rate any film which they had seen on a scale of 1 (great) to 3 (awful). The list contained a selection of titles from the 'top 100' videos of September 1983. These titles included 29 videos that had been given an '18' certificate by the British Board of Film Censors. The list also contained 34 titles of violent horror videos that had been found obscene under the Obscene Publications Act, 1959 or were at that time currently the subject of legal proceedings or being considered for prosecution by the Director of Public Prosecutions. We have called this list 'the DPP's list'.

The following table shows the percentage of children and the percentage of parents who have seen each of these videos on the DPP's list.

Table 5.4 *Percentage of parents and percentage of children who have seen each individual film on the DPP's list*

Film Title on the DPP's list	% Parents	% Children	Film Title on the DPP's list	% Parents	% Children
Absurd	2.7	2.5	Evil Speak	3.7	2.8
Beast in Heat	1.7	1.2	Faces of Death	1.7	1.7
Blood Feast	5.2	3.9	House on the Edge of the Park	2.4	2.9
The Bogey Man	11.6	10.2	I Spit on Your Grave	18.2	7.3
The Burning	15.7	10.0	Last House on the Left	6.9	5.8
Cannibal Apocalypse	10.2	4.8	The Living Dead	23.0	12.6
Cannibal Ferox	3.8	2.5	Mardi Gras Massacre	2.7	0.8
Cannibal Holocaust	8.0	3.7	Nightmares in a Damaged Brain	4.1	2.6
Cannibal Man	4.2	3.9	Night of the Demon	7.1	6.7
Cannibal Terror	3.5	3.0	Possession	6.9	1.9
Contamination	3.7	1.7	Pranks	1.8	1.4
Dead and Buried	7.3	6.6	The Slayer	3.3	4.3
Death Trap	9.2	7.9	Snuff	3.9	2.8
Don't Go in the House	5.1	4.4	SS Experiment Camp	6.0	2.9
Don't Go in the Woods Alone	5.6	4.4	Zombie Creeping Flesh	14.2	9.0
Driller Killer	9.0	6.2	Zombie Flesh-Eaters	23.4	15.9
The Evil Dead	23.4	15.7	Zombie Terror	9.5	5.4

The most popular films with the *parents and the children alike* were *The Evil Dead, Zombie Flesh-Eaters* and *The Living Dead*. These films have been seen by a higher percentage of parents than children in this sample. Nevertheless, the same films tend to be popular with both the parents and the children which raises the question whether these videos were viewed as a family, or whether the videos were hired by the parents for their own viewing but the children played the video without the parents' knowledge.

The following table shows the percentage of parents and the percentage of children who have seen none, one or more, or four or more videos on the DPP's list.

Table 5.5 *Percentage of parents and percentage of children who have seen none, one or more, or four or more videos on the DPP's list*

%	Number of films on the DPP's list seen		
	None	One or more	Four or more
Children	63.3	36.7	15.5
Parents	54.1	45.9	25.1

NB The figures for seeing four or more videos are included in the figures for seeing one or more videos since a child who has seen four videos has obviously seen more than one video.

It seems *that many more parents than children in this sample have seen videos on the DPP's list*. Over 45% of the parents have seen at least one 'video nasty' and over a quarter of the parents have seen at least 4 of these films.

The overall percentage of children in this sample who have seen at least one violent video is 36.7%. This is in fact lower than the comparable figure in the National Viewers' Survey (45.5%). However, when one takes into account that far fewer children have VCRs in their own homes in this sample and that fewer children watch video films at friends' houses it is clear that the opportunities for these children to see such videos could be somewhat smaller than in the general survey. In the light of this, the figure of 36.7% seems remarkably high. This could indicate a degree of conscious preference.

The following table gives a breakdown by age and sex of the percentage of children in this sample who have seen at least one video on the DPP's list.

Table 5.6 *Percentage of children who have seen one or more videos on the DPP's list by age and sex*

		Age (Years) of children					
		7–8	9–10	11–12	13–14	15–16	All ages
Sex	*Boys*	18.5	38.0	32.9	65.6	78.1	39.2
	Girls	15.2	13.0	38.5	58.7	69.8	34.1
	Both	16.9	26.6	35.1	61.9	73.3	36.7

There is a very pronounced difference in the number of children in this sample who have seen one or more violent videos according to their age. Less than 20% of 7- to 8-year-olds have seen a 'video nasty' whereas over 70% of 15- to 16-year-olds have watched such a video film. **Exposure to violent videos increases steadily with age in this underprivileged sample**, in contrast to the National Viewers' Survey which shows a peak at the age of 13 to 14 years for exposure to 'video nasties', with a falling off thereafter.

This increase in the watching of violent videos with age could stem from the trend shown in the earlier tables for watching videos at a friend's or relative's house. Since very few children actually have VCRs in their own homes (and these figures do not show any pattern due to the age of the child) it seems likely that the majority of the children who have seen a 'video nasty' have done so at a friend's house.

Sex also seems to be a relevant variable in this underprivileged sample in that generally more boys have seen violent videos than girls. More 11- to 12-year-old girls, however, have seen violent videos than have boys of that age.

The figure below shows the difference between the two samples in the percentage of children who have seen at least one video on the DPP's list according to the age and sex of the children. The graph shows that although fewer children in the NSPCC sample have seen a 'video nasty' in the younger age groups than children of the same age in the National Viewers' Survey, the positions are reversed in the older age groups where more children in the NSPCC sample have seen a 'video nasty' than have children in the National Viewers' Survey.

Fig. 5.2 *Percentage of children in each sample who have seen one or more videos on the DPPs list by age and sex.*

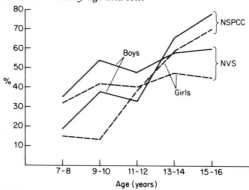

The following table gives a breakdown by age and sex of the percentage of children who have seen four or more videos on the DPP's list.

Table 5.7 *Percentage of children who have seen four or more videos on the DPP's list by age and sex*

		Age (Years) of children					
		7–8	9–10	11–12	13–14	15–16	All ages
	Boys	2.8	10.9	15.9	37.7	53.1	17.6
Sex	*Girls*	2.2	2.6	7.7	30.2	39.5	13.2
	Both	2.5	7.1	11.9	34.1	45.3	15.5

It was felt that, whereas children (or parents) who have seen one video on the DPP's list may have done so accidentally, those who have seen four or more have deliberately chosen to view this type of video.

A very similar pattern can be seen in this table as was seen in the table showing the number of children who have seen one or more videos on the DPP's list. The overall percentage of 15.5 children having seen four or more violent videos is again lower than the comparable figure in the general survey. The explanation that these children have less opportunity to watch videos may still hold.

The difference in exposure to videos on the DPP's list according to age can again be seen very clearly. Only 2·5% of 7 to 8 year-olds have seen four or more while over 45% of 15 to 16 year-olds have seen four or more of these videos. There is a steady increase in exposure with age and **by the age of 15 to 16 almost half of the children in this age group in this underprivileged sample have seen four or more obscene videos**.

The difference in viewing patterns between boys and girls is again very clear with more boys of all ages having seen four or more videos on the DPP's list than girls of the corresponding ages.

The following table shows the percentage of children who have a VCR at home and who have seen videos at a friend's or relative's house who have seen one or more, and four or more videos on the DPP's list.

Table 5.8   *Percentage of children who have seen none, one or more, or four or more videos on the DPP's list according to whether they have seen a video at a friend's or relative's house and whether they have a VCR at home*

	No. of DPP films seen		
	0	*1+*	*4+*
All children in sample	63.3	36.7	15.5
Children who have seen a video at a friend's	55.0	45.0	19.8
Children who have a VCR at home	43.9	56.1	25.5
Children who have seen a video at a friend's **AND** have a VCR at home	36.3	63.7	31.9

The above table shows that 36.7% and 15.5% of all children in this sample have seen one or more, and four or more videos on the DPP's list, respectively.

These figures increase to 45.0% and 19.8% respectively when only those children who have seen a video at a friend's house are taken into account.

Thus, watching videos at a friend's house not only increases the opportunity for children to view violent videos, it actually increases the likelihood of them doing so.

Similarly, having a VCR at home increases the likelihood of children seeing a violent video. 56.1% of children who have a VCR at home have seen a 'video nasty' and over 25% have seen four or more.

When only children who have a VCR at home **and** who have seen videos at a friend's or relative's house are taken into account, Table 5.8 shows that 63.7% of children have seen one or more videos on the DPP's list, while 31.9% of children have seen four or more such videos.

Given that the vast majority of children who have seen a video will have seen that video at home (if they have a VCR) or at a friend's or relative's house, we can assume that the children in the general survey and in the underprivileged sample who answered 'Yes' to both of these questions had equal opportunities to see a 'video nasty'.

Although the figures in the two samples for children seeing one or more videos on the DPP's list when they have had 'equal opportunity' to do so are remarkably close (thus confirming each other as a reliable result), slightly fewer children in the underprivileged sample (63.7%) seem to have seen this type of film than children in the general survey (64.9%). This can also be seen in the four-or-more figures in that over 37% of children in the general survey have seen four or more 'video nasties' whereas less than 32% of children in the underprivileged sample who have a VCR at home and have seen a video at a friend's house have seen four or more 'video nasties'.

These figures are directly comparable with the figures in the general survey since they overcome any 'opportunity' differences between the two groups.

In the list of video film titles that was given in the parents' and children's questionnaires there were 29 '18' rated films now available in video form. The following table shows the percentage of parents and children who have seen each of these '18' rated video films. It needs to be stressed that these are films (formerly 'X') which no person under 18-years-old would be permitted to view in a public cinema.

Table 5.9 *Percentage of parents and percentage of children who have seen each individual '18' rated film*

'18' Rated Film Title	% Parents	% Children	'18' Rated Film Title	% Parents	% Children
An American Werewolf in London	22.5	21.9	Mad Max	21.4	22.3
Amityville II – The Possession	15.2	6.0	Mad Max II	12.8	15.0
The Border	2.5	1.8	Midnight Express	13.1	7.3
Bronx Warriors	9.5	9.0	One Flew Over the Cuckoo's Nest	19.2	8.2
Caligula	5.6	1.7	Piranha	27.1	27.3
Cat People	3.1	2.1	Poltergeist	21.4	13.6
			Private Lessons	10.6	6.0

Table 5.9 *continued*

'18' Rated Film Title	% Parents	% Children	'18' Rated Film Title	% Parents	% Children
Confessions of a Driving			Q – The Winged Serpent	1.7	0.7
Instructor	13.2	6.0	The Sentinel	4.1	1.4
Death Wish II	21.4	10.5	Sharkey's Machine	2.9	2.6
Fanny Hill	3.3	1.5	The Shining	16.1	7.8
Fort Apache – The Bronx	12.8	7.5	Texas Chain Saw Massacre	23.0	12.2
Friday 13th Part 2	27.5	14.4	The Thing	14.1	12.5
Funhouse	3.5	3.6	Vigilante	6.5	1.8
The Howling	13.5	8.6	Wolfen	2.9	2.1
The Long Riders	5.2	7.8			

The most popular film in this list is *Piranha* with over 27% of both parents and children having seen this film. *An American Werewolf in London* and *Mad Max* also seem to be quite popular, with approximately 22% of both parents and children having seen each of these films. The most popular film with the parents is *Friday the 13th Part 2*, with 27.5% having seen this film. Only 14.4% of the children have seen this film.

Fig. 5.3 *Percentage of children who have seen one or more videos on the DPP's list by VCR at home and video at a friend's house.*

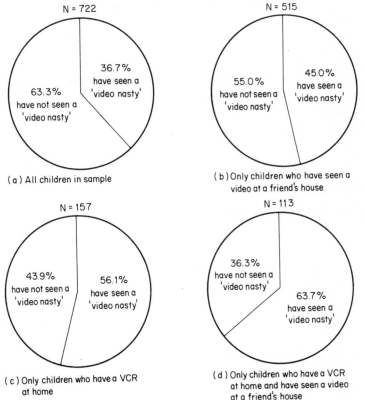

(a) All children in sample

(b) Only children who have seen a video at a friend's house

(c) Only children who have a VCR at home

(d) Only children who have a VCR at home and have seen a video at a friend's house

Fig. 5.3 (a) on the previous page shows that 36.7% of all children in the under-privileged sample have seen at least one video on the DPP's list, while 63.7% have seen none. Fig. 5.3 (b) shows that 45% of the children in this sample who have seen a video at a friend's house, have seen a 'video nasty' while 55% have not. Fig. 5.3 (c) shows that 56% of children who have a VCR at home have seen a 'video nasty' while 44% have not. Fig. 5.3 (d) shows that out of those children who have a VCR at home and have seen a video at a friend's house, 64% have seen a 'video nasty' while only 36% have not.

The following table shows the percentage of parents and the percentage of children who have seen none, one or more, or four or more '18' rated video films.

Table 5.10   *Percentage of parents and percentage of children who have seen none, one or more or four or more '18' rated video films*

%	None	One or more	Four or more
	No. of '18' rated films seen		
Children	49.9	50.1	24.2
Parents	40.9	59.1	35.0

The figures show that more parents than children have seen '18' rated video films, the difference being approximately 10%. 59% of parents have seen at least one '18' rated video while 35% have seen four or more '18' films.

The table above shows that half of the children in this sample have seen at least one '18' rated video film and almost a quarter have seen four or more '18' certificate films. These percentages are, in fact, lower than the comparable figures in the National Viewers' Survey. However, the smaller opportunities for the children in this sample to see any video film at all could be a causal factor in these lower figures.

The following table gives a breakdown by age and sex of the percentage of children in this sample who have seen one or more '18' rated video films.

Table 5.11 *Percentage of children who have seen one or more '18' rated video films by age and sex*

| | | Age (Years) of children | | | | | |
		7–8	9–10	11–12	13–14	15–16	All ages
Sex	*Boys*	27.8	57.6	52.4	73.8	87.5	53.1
	Girls	25.0	41.6	52.3	63.5	74.4	47.4
	Both	26.4	50.3	52.3	68.3	80.0	50.1

It is clear from the above table that 50% of the children in this sample have seen at least one '18' rated video film. Yet these children are aged between 7 and 16 years and would not legally be allowed to see these films in a cinema.

The table also shows that there is a dramatic increase in the numbers of children who have seen an '18' film according to age. Thus, many more older children have seen an '18' film than the younger children and by the time they are 15- to 16-years-old 80% of this age group have seen an '18' rated video film.

The table also shows that more boys than girls have seen one or more '18' video films. This is true throughout all the age groups.

The table below shows the percentage of children of both sexes and in each age group who have seen four or more '18' rated video films.

Table 5.12 *Percentage of children who have seen four or more '18' rated video films by age and sex*

| | | Age (Years) of children | | | | | |
		7–8	9–10	11–12	13–14	15–16	All ages
Sex	*Boys*	9.3	20.7	25.6	44.3	71.9	26.7
	Girls	7.6	6.5	21.5	38.1	53.5	21.5
	Both	8.5	14.2	23.8	41.3	61.3	24.2

Almost one quarter of the children in this sample have seen four or more '18' rated videos. This is, however, lower than the comparable figure in the general survey since almost 30% of those children have seen at least four '18' rated films.

Age is once again a relevant factor in the viewing of '18' rated films by children. Sex, too, is an important factor, with more boys tending to watch '18' films than girls. Over 70% of 15- to 16-year-old boys in the sample have seen at least four '18' rated films on video. This figure is much higher than the comparable figure in the general survey. Less than 50% of 15- to 16-year-old boys in the general survey have seen four or more '18' rated videos.

The graph below shows the upward trend with age in the percentage of children in the two samples who have seen at least one '18' rated video film. It also clearly shows the difference been the sexes in watching these videos.

Fig. 5.4   *Percentage of children in each sample who have seen one or more '18' rated video films by age and sex.*

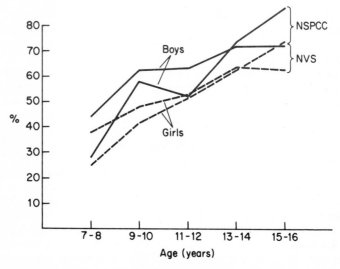

The table on the next page shows the percentage of children of all ages who have a VCR at home and have seen a video at a friend's or relative's house, who have seen one or more, and four or more '18' rated video films.

Table 5.13 *Percentage of children who have seen none, one or more, or four or more '18' rated video films according to whether they have seen a video at a friend's house and whether they have a VCR at home*

	No. of '18' rated films seen		
	0	*1+*	*4+*
All children in sample	49.9	50.1	24.2
Children who have seen a video at a friend's	38.8	61.2	30.5
Children who have a VCR at home	28.0	72.0	45.2
Children who have seen a video at a friend's **AND** have a VCR at home	19.5	80.5	53.1

The table confirms that 50% and 24% of all the children in the whole sample have seen one or more and four or more '18' rated video films, respectively. These figures, however, increase to 61% and 30% respectively when only children who have seen a video at a friend's house are taken into account. Similarly, these figures for watching one or more and four or more '18' rated video films increase to 72% and 45% when only children who have a VCR at home are taken into account.

The table also shows that **over 80% of children in this sample who have a VCR at home and who have seen videos at a friend's house have seen at least one '18' rated film,** and over half of these children with maximum viewing opportunity have seen four or more '18' rated films.

The diagrams on the following page illustrate clearly the percentage of children in this under-privileged sample who have seen at least one '18' rated video film according to whether or not they have a VCR at home and have seen a video film at a friend's house. Fig 5.5 (a) shows that half of all the children in this sample have seen an '18' rated video film while Fig. 5.5 (d) shows that over 80% of those children in the sample who have a VCR at home and have seen a video at a friend's house, have seen such a video.

Fig. 5.5   *Percentage of children who have seen one or more '18' rated video films by VCR at home and video at a friend's house.*

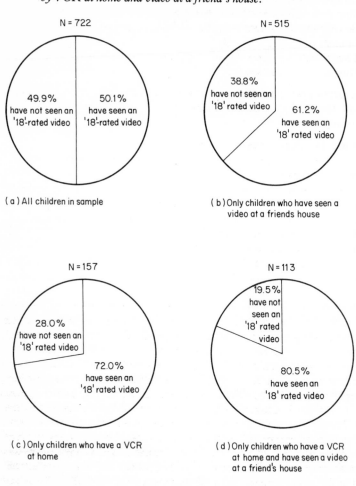

(a) All children in sample

(b) Only children who have seen a video at a friends house

(c) Only children who have a VCR at home

(d) Only children who have a VCR at home and have seen a video at a friend's house

How Concerned are the Parents?

Every parent through the parents' questionnaire was asked to assess their reaction to a situation in which they discovered that their child had seen, at a friend's house, a video film that they considered to be unsuitable. This, of course, assumes that the parents would regard some films as unsuitable for children. The parents were asked to indicate in which of the following ways they would react:

1 Report the incident to the police.
2 Go and see the parents.
3 Stop your child from visiting the house.
4 Be very angry at the incident but decide not to do anything.
5 Contact your MP.
6 There would be no need to do anything.
7 Discuss the incident with your child.

The parents were allowed to indicate more than one reaction. The table below shows the percentage of parents who would react in each of the following ways.

Table 5.14 *Action chosen by parents*

No.	*Action*	*%*
1	Report the incident to the police	6.7
2	Go and see the parents	61.0
3	Stop your child from visiting the house	41.2
4	Be angry, but do nothing	4.1
5	Contact your MP	0.8
6	No need to do anything	2.7
7	Discuss the incident with your child	37.4

As with the National Viewers' Survey the second, third and seventh responses were the most popular, although the parents in this sample seemed to be more keen on actually visiting the parents than in the 'general' survey. While 70% of the parents in the National Viewers' Survey would discuss the incident with their child, only 37% of the parents in this underprivileged sample would talk to the child. The parents are much more likely to go and see the parents of the other child or to stop their child from visiting the house.

6.7% of the parents in this sample said they would report the incident to the police, while only 1.8% of the parents in the National Viewers' Survey chose this response. On the whole, **the parents in this sample seem to be significantly more 'authoritarian'** than the parents in the 'general' survey.

The following figure shows the difference between the NSPCC sample and the National Viewers' Survey in the percentage of parents who chose each of the seven responses. The percentages of parents choosing each response are fairly similar except that many more parents in the under-privileged sample would 'Report the incident to the police', or 'Go and see the parents' while many more parents in the National Viewers' Survey would discuss the incident with their child.

Fig. 5.6   *Percentage of parents in each sample choosing each response.*

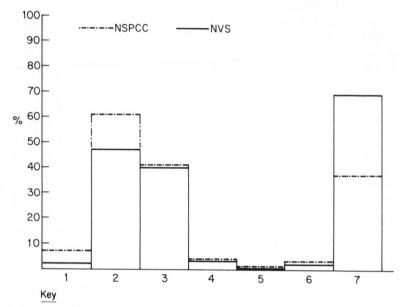

Key

1 = Report the incident to the police

2 = Go and see the parents

3 = Stop your child from visiting the house

4 = Be angry but do nothing

5 = Contact your MP

6 = No need to do anything

7 = Discuss the incident with your child

The parents could choose more than one action if they so wished and Table 5.15 shows the combination of actions chosen by the parents in their response.

Table 5.15 *Percentage of parents who would choose each combination of responses*

Response	%	Response	%	Response	%
2 alone	25.4	2+3	8.9	3+7	3.7
3 alone	16.5	2+3+7	8.8	6 alone	2.4
2+7	13.6	7 alone	8.0	miscellaneous	12.9

The highest response is 2 alone, followed by 3 alone and a combination of 2 and 7. While the highest response in the National Viewers' Survey was 7 alone and 7 appeared in each of the four highest responses, 7 alone is the sixth highest response in the underprivileged sample and 7 appears in only one of the four highest responses. These families who are visited by the officers of the NSPCC appear not to value discussion between parents and children as much as the parents in the general survey. They seem to prefer to protect their children without giving reasons. This may be due to either the lower age of the parents and the children in the underprivileged sample, or the lower social class of the families in the underprivileged sample when compared with the National Viewers' Survey.

In the parents' questionnaire a selection of television programmes was presented and the parents were asked to indicate at what age they would allow their children to watch the programmes.

The following tables show the percentage of parents who would allow their children to watch each of these television programmes at different ages.

Table 5.16 *Percentage of parents allowing their children to watch different television programmes only when they are over certain ages*

	Age (Years) of Children					
Name of programme	Any age	Over 5	Over 10	Over 12	Over 15	Over 18
Minder	20.3	14.6	19.1	11.5	8.5	2.1
Hill Street Blues	13.1	6.9	14.6	13.6	14.1	3.8
War news	14.5	6.0	14.5	12.7	11.4	9.4
The Professionals	20.7	12.3	20.0	14.0	7.7	2.2
The Sweeney	18.2	9.0	17.5	15.2	11.1	2.7

Table 5.16   *continued*

Name of programme	Age (Years) of Children					
	Any age	Over 5	Over 10	Over 12	Over 15	Over 18
Benny Hill	20.4	13.9	16.2	12.0	8.2	4.8
Carry On Films	38.4	17.6	14.0	7.5	3.9	2.5
Tom and Jerry	92.2	3.9	0.3	0.0	0.0	0.0
The 'A' Team	40.3	24.1	13.2	4.4	4.1	0.8
Play for Today	12.0	5.4	14.1	14.6	13.5	4.3
Kenny Everett	18.7	12.5	14.1	11.8	9.0	6.9
Dallas	28.8	14.8	17.0	8.2	3.8	2.6
Grange Hill	47.7	23.7	9.2	3.4	0.7	0.7
Dukes of Hazzard	51.2	22.6	10.7	1.3	0.8	0.4

The programmes were chosen to give an assessment of the parents' reactions to programmes containing scenes of violence and others containing sexual innuendo. With the exception of the responses to *Tom and Jerry* and war news **a much higher percentage of parents in this sample would allow their children to watch the programmes at any age** than the parents in the National Viewers' Survey.

Fewer parents in the underprivileged sample would restrict children under 12-years-old from watching any of the programmes in the list when compared with the restrictions placed on children by the parents in the National Viewers' Survey. For example, 18% of the parents in this sample would allow their children to watch *The Sweeney* at any age and only 15% of parents in this sample would restrict viewing of *The Sweeney* to children over 12-years-old. The comparable figures in the National Survey are only 9% of parents allowing their children to watch *The Sweeney* at any age and 22% restricting watching to children over 12-years-old.

What do the Parents Think?

Also in the parents' questionnaire, a number of statements were put to the parents in this sample and they were asked to rate their agreement or disagreement with them. The following table shows the percentage of parents who agreed or disagreed with the following statements. This is the same list included in the National Viewers' Survey questionnaire, as given in Chapter 4.

1 Left to themselves children will only watch what is good for them.
2 It doesn't matter what children watch.
3 Any film which is considered not to be obscene should be available to adults from their video library.
4 Only films which have been passed by the British Board of Film Censors for public exhibition should be available in video libraries.
5 Society has a duty to protect children from uncensored video films.
6 Parents should have the final responsibility as to what their children should, or should not, watch.
7 There are too many children's programmes on television.
8 There should be a separate channel for children's television.
9 Children watch too much television.
10 Parents allow their children to watch too much television.

NB   The statements in the above list are not in the same order as they were in the questionnaire.

Table 5.17   *Parents' opinions on these statements*
(The rows do not add up to 100% because some parents did not give their opinion on some of the statements)

Statement Number	% Agree Strongly	% Agree	% Neither Agree nor Disagree	% Disagree	% Disagree Strongly
1	2.5	18.2	8.9	44.3	20.0
2	1.8	3.9	4.2	43.3	38.8
3	10.3	57.3	14.4	7.5	2.9
4	11.4	40.7	16.3	19.3	4.7
5	39.7	43.7	4.1	4.2	1.8
6	38.6	48.9	3.3	3.9	0.8
7	1.8	5.2	21.8	48.9	16.2
8	15.8	38.8	11.4	24.8	3.4
9	10.6	34.4	21.7	25.5	1.4
10	8.4	32.2	24.3	27.6	2.5

Over 20% of parents in this sample agree with the statement 'left to themselves children will only watch what is good for them' while only 12.5% of parents in the National Viewers' Survey agreed with this statement. Similarly, only 64% disagreed with this statement in this sample, while almost 80% disagreed in the National Viewers' Survey. The following table shows the differences in agreement and disagreement between the two surveys.

Table 5.18 *Differences between the surveys in the parents' opinions on the
statements*

Statement Number	Opinions			
	% Agree		% Disagree	
	NSPCC	NVS	NSPCC	NVS
1	20.7	12.5	64.3	79.1
2	5.7	3.2	82.1	91.5
3	67.6	68.2	10.4	11.2
4	52.1	59.2	24.0	24.9
5	83.4	90.2	6.0	3.8
6	87.5	89.2	4.7	4.8
7	7.0	4.7	65.1	65.3
8	54.6	37.7	28.2	44.0
9	45.0	58.9	26.9	16.9
10	40.6	54.3	30.1	20.0

Do Parents Influence their Children?

In order to assess the influence of the parents' attitudes on the children's
viewing patterns, the individual parents' and children's questionnaires were
matched. In this way the data from the children and the parents in the same
family could be studied together.

There are 687 matched pairs (parents and children) in this matched
sample. That is, there are 687 children aged 7 to 16 years. The data obtained
from the parents of these children has been matched with the 687 children.
However, in some cases there may be more than one child in the same family
with the same parents. In these cases the parents' data has been duplicated to
be matched with each of their children.

A good example of the influence of parental attitudes on children's viewing
patterns can be seen in the following table which shows the percentage of
children who have seen none, one or more, or four or more videos on the
DPP's list according to their parents' reactions to them seeing an 'unsuitable'
video film at a friend's house.

Table 5.19 *Percentage of children who have seen none, one or more, or four or more videos on the DPP's list according to parents' reactions*

	No. DPPs seen by children		
Actions	*0*	*1+*	*4+*
Report to police	66.7	33.3	13.7
Go and see the parents	69.9	30.1	10.8
Stop child visiting	65.7	34.3	14.4
Be angry, but do nothing	65.6	34.4	18.8
Contact your MP	0.0	0.0	0.0
No need to do anything	44.4	55.6	27.8
Discuss with child	64.4	35.6	18.5

Over 55% of the children whose parents thought 'there would be no need to do anything' had seen at least one 'video nasty' and over a quarter of these children had seen four or more videos on the DPP's list. Only 30% of the children whose parents would 'go and see the parents' had seen a 'video nasty' and less than 11% had seen four or more of these violent video films. There are no parents in this matched sample who would react by contacting their MP.

The following table shows the percentage of children who have seen none, one or more, four or more '18' rated video films according to their parents' reactions to their child seeing an 'unsuitable' video at a friend's house.

Table 5.20 *Percentage of children who have seen none, one or more, or four or more '18' rated videos according to their parents' reactions*

	No. '18's seen		
Actions	*0*	*1+*	*4+*
Report to police	52.9	47.1	19.6
Go and see the parents	55.1	44.9	18.9
Stop child visiting	53.8	46.2	20.3
Be angry, but do nothing	56.3	43.7	25.0
Contact your MP	0.0	0.0	0.0
No need to do anything	38.9	61.1	38.9
Discuss with child	50.7	49.3	24.7

The table above shows a similar pattern to the previous table for children watching films on the DPP's list. In this table the percentage of children who have seen an '18' rated film is much higher for the children whose parents thought 'there would be no need to do anything' than for the children whose parents responded in any of the other ways. The lowest percentage of children seeing one or more '18' film seems to be for the children whose parents chose the apparently 'irrational' response of being angry but deciding not to do anything. However, for the 'heavy' viewing of four or more '18' rated films the children whose parents would 'go and see the parents' or 'report the incident to the police' are the least likely to have seen more than 3 '18' rated video films.

One of the most interesting comparisons we can make is between the viewing patterns of the parents and of the children. Do the preferences of the parents influence the type of films that the children watch? The following table shows the percentage of children in this sample who have seen none, one or more, four or more videos on the DPP's list.

Table 5.21   *Percentage of children who have seen none, one or more, or four or more videos on the DPP's list regardless of how many their parents have seen*

	No. of 'video nasties' seen by child		
	0	*1+*	*4+*
%	63.3	36.7	15.5

These figures were given earlier in this chapter and refer to the viewing patterns of all the children in the sample regardless of whether their parents have seen any 'video nasties'. These figures may be taken as the average viewing figures for the children in this sample and will form the basis for comparison with the figures in the following tables.

The following table shows the percentage of children who have seen none, one or more, four or more videos on the DPP's list when their parents have seen NO videos on the DPP's list.

Table 5.22   *Percentage of children who have seen none, one or more, or four or more videos on the DPP's list when their parents have seen NO films on the DPP's list*

	No. of 'video nasties' seen by child		
	0	*1+*	*4+*
%	76.0	24.0	9.1

Over three-quarters of the children whose parents have seen no videos on the DPP's list have themselves seen no videos on the DPP's list. Only 24% of these children have seen a 'video nasty' and only 9% have seen four or more 'video nasties'. These figures are much lower than the comparable figures in the whole sample for viewing one or more (36.7%) and four or more (15.5%) 'video nasties'. **These figures show that when the parents do not watch violent videos their children are also much less likely to do so.**

The following table shows the percentage of children who have seen none, one or more, or four or more videos on the DPP's list when their parents have seen at least one video on the DPP's list.

Table 5.23   *Percentage of children who have seen none, one or more, or four or more videos on the DPP's list when their parents have seen at least ONE video on the DPP's list*

	No. of 'video nasties' seen by child		
	0	*1+*	*4+*
%	45.9	54.1	25.4

The table above shows that 54% of the children whose parents have seen a 'video nasty' have themselves seen a 'video nasty' and over 25% of these children have seen four or more 'video nasties'. These figures are quite considerably higher than the average figures for viewing one or more and four or more 'video nasties' (36.7% and 15.5% respectively). The figures in the table above illustrate the influence of the parents' viewing patterns on their children's viewing patterns. **When the parents watch violent films on video the children are also much more likely to do so.**

The following table shows the percentage of children who have seen none, one or more, or four or more videos on the DPP's list when their parents have seen four or more videos on the DPP's list.

Table 5.24   *Percentage of children who have seen none, one or more, or four or more videos on the DPP's list when their parents have seen at least FOUR videos on the DPP's list*

	No. of 'video nasties' seen by child		
	0	*1+*	*4+*
%	43.0	57.0	30.9

Only 43% of the children whose parents have seen four or more videos on the DPP's list have seen none of these videos. This is much lower than either the average viewing figures for all the children in the sample who have seen no 'video nasties' (63.3%) or for the percentage of children who have seen no 'video nasties' when their parents have seen none of these films (76.0%).

The table above also shows that 57% of the children whose parents have seen four or more 'video nasties' have seen at least one 'video nasty' and over 30% of these children have themselves seen four or more of these videos.

The above tables show very clearly that the more violent video films that are watched by the parents, the greater the likelihood that the children of those parents will watch violent video films too. **The viewing patterns of the parents are one of the most influential factors affecting the type of films that the children will watch.**

Fig. 5.7   *Percentage of children who have seen one or more videos on the DPP's list according to how many videos on the DPP's list have been seen by their parents.*

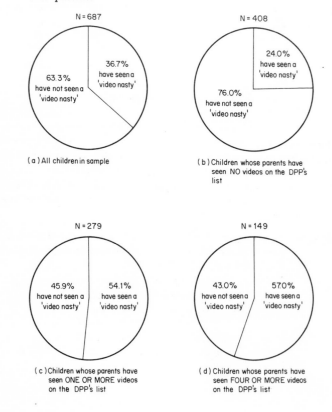

N = 687

36.7% have seen a 'video nasty'

63.3% have not seen a 'video nasty'

(a) All children in sample

N = 408

24.0% have seen a 'video nasty'

76.0% have not seen a 'video nasty'

(b) Children whose parents have seen NO videos on the DPP's list

N = 279

45.9% have not seen a 'video nasty'

54.1% have seen a 'video nasty'

(c) Children whose parents have seen ONE OR MORE videos on the DPP's list

N = 149

43.0% have not seen a 'video nasty'

57.0% have seen a 'video nasty'

(d) Children whose parents have seen FOUR OR MORE videos on the DPP's list

Fig. 5.7 (a) on the previous page shows that 36.7% of all the children in this underprivileged sample have seen at least one video on the DPP's list, while 63.3% have seen at least one video on the DPP's list, while 63.3% have seen none. Fig 5.7 (b) and (c) illustrate clearly how the percentage of children who have seen a 'video nasty' increases from 24% when the children's parents have seen no 'video nasties' to 54% when the children's parents have seen at least one 'video nasty'. Fig. 5.7 (d) shows that the percentage increases even more when the parents have seen four or more of these videos. The viewing patterns of the parents are clearly an important influence on the viewing patterns of the children.

The following tables show the percentage of children who have seen none, one or more, or four or more '18' rated video films according to how many of these films their parents have seen. Again, we will first look at the percentage of children in the total sample who have seen none, one or more, or four or more '18' rated video films regardless of whether their parents have seen any of these films or not.

Table 5.25   *Percentage of children who have seen none, one or more, or four or more '18' rated films*

	No. of '18' films seen by child		
	0	*1+*	*4+*
%	49.9	50.1	24.2

The figures in the table above may be taken as the average viewing figures for all the children in the sample for '18' rated films. These figures will form the basis for comparison with the figures in the following tables.

The following table shows the percentage of children who have seen none, one or more, four or more '18' rated video films when their parents have seen NO '18' rated films.

Table 5.26   *Percentage of children who have seen none, one or more, or four of more '18' rated films when their parents have seen No '18' rated films*

	No. of '18' films seen by child		
	0	*1+*	*4+*
%	66.7	33.3	12.3

Two-thirds of the children whose parents have seen none of the '18' rated video films on the list have themselves seen none of these films. This is a much higher figure than the average for children having seen no '18' rated films (49.9%). Table 5.26 also shows that only 33% and 12% of children whose parents have not seen an '18' rated film have seen one or more and four or more of these films respectively. These figures are considerably lower than the average figures for children viewing '18' rated films (50.1% and 24.2% for one or more and four or more respectively).

The following table shows the percentage of children who have seen none, one or more, four or more '18' rated video films when their parents have seen at least one '18' rated video film.

Table 5.27   *Percentage of children who have seen none, one or more, or four or more '18' rated films when their parents have seen at least ONE '18' rated film*

	No. of '18' films seen by child		
	0	*1+*	*4+*
%	35.1	64.9	34.3

The table above shows that only 35% of these children whose parents have seen at least one '18' rated video film have seen no '18' rated video films, while 65% of these children have seen at least one '18' rated film and over 34% have seen four or more '18' rated films. These figures, when compared with the average viewing figures for '18' rated films, illustrate that the children whose parents have seen '18' rated films are more likely to have seen '18' rated video films themselves.

The following table shows the percentage of children who have seen none, one or more, or four or more '18' rated video films when their parents have seen at least four '18' rated films.

Table 5.28   *Percentage of children who have seen none, one or more, or four or more '18' rated films when their parents have seen at least FOUR '18' rated films*

	No. of '18' films seen by child		
	0	*1+*	*4+*
%	27.6	72.4	43.8

Table 5.28 shows that only 27.6% of the children with parents who have seen at least four '18' rated videos have seen no '18' rated films on the list. Over 72% of these children, however, whose parents have seen four or more '18' rated videos have seen at least one '18' rated film and over 43% of these children have themselves seen at least four '18' rated video films.

The table also shows that the children with parents who enjoy watching '18' rated video films are more likely to watch this type of film themselves.

Fig. 5.8 *Percentage of children who have seen one or more '18' rated video films according to how many '18' rated video films have been seen by their parents.*

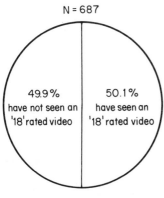

(a) All children in sample

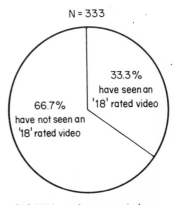

(b) Children whose parents have seen NO '18' rated videos

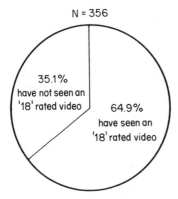

(c) Children whose parents have seen ONE OR MORE '18' rated videos

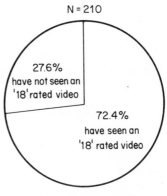

(d) Children whose parents have seen FOUR OR MORE '18' rated videos

The charts on the previous page clearly illustrate how dramatically the percentage of children who have seen and '18' rated video is influenced by the number of '18' rated video films seen by their parents.

The above tables and figures relating to '18' rated video viewing patterns confirm the results of the figures for viewing videos on the DPP's list.

Thus we may conclude that the viewing patterns of the parents are clearly a very influential factor when considering the viewing patterns of children. **Children with parents who watch a high number of violent videos are more likely to watch a high number of violent videos themselves than are children with parents who do not watch any violent video films.**

Summary

1 Only 22% of families in this sample own or rent a VCR, compared with the national average for VCR ownership in families with school-age children of 41%.

2 71% of children in this sample have seen a video film at a friend's or relative's house, while only 57% of parents knew, or admitted that their children have seen a video at a friend's or relative's house.

3 36.7% of children in this sample have seen at least one video on the DPP's list while 15.5% have seen at least four of these films.

4 46% of the parents in this sample have seen at least one video on the DPP's list, with 25% having seen four or more of these films.

5 The *same* films on the DPP's list (ie *The Evil Dead*, *Zombie Flesh-Eaters* and *The Living Dead*) and the same '18' rated films (ie *Piranha, An American Werewolf in London* and *Mad Max*) tend to be popular with *both* parents and children.

6 Less than 20% of the 7-to 8-year-old children in this sample have seen one or more videos on the DPP's list, whereas over 70% of the 15- to 16-year-old children have seen at least one of these films.

7 Similarly, less than 3% of the 7- to 8-year-old children in this sample have seen four or more 'video nasties' while over 45% of the 15- to 16-year-olds have seen at least four of these films.

8 45% of all the children in this sample who have seen a video at a friend's or relative's house have seen at least one 'video nasty'.

9 56% of all the children in this sample who have a VCR at home have seen at least one 'video nasty'.

10 Over 63% of all the children who have seen a video at a friend's or relative's house and have a VCR at home have seen at least one 'video nasty'.

11 50% of all the children in this sample have seen at least one of the '18' rated video films on our list and 24% have seen at least four of these films.

12 59% of all the parents in this sample have seen at least one of the '18' rated video films on our list, and 35% have seen at least four of these films.

13 There is a very clear difference in the percentage of children in this sample who have seen '18' rated films according to both the age and sex of the children.

14 61% of all the children in this sample who have seen a video film at a friend's or relative's house have seen at least one '18' rated film.

15 72% of all the children in this sample who have a VCR at home have seen at least one '18' rated film.

16 Over 80% of all the children in this sample who have seen a video at a friend's or relative's house and have a VCR at home have seen at least one '18' rated film.

17 The majority of parents in this sample indicated that they would 'Go and see the parents' if they found that their child had seen an 'unsuitable' video at a friend's house. Only 37% of parents in this sample would discuss the incident with their child while 70% of the parents in the National Viewers' Survey would discuss it with their child.

18 Only 30% of the children of those parents who would 'Go and see the parents' have seen a 'video nasty' whereas over 55% of the children of those parents who thought 'There would be no need to do anything' have seen a 'video nasty'.

19 The viewing patterns of the parents are a major influence on the viewing patterns of the children.

20 Only 24% of the children whose parents have seen no videos on the DPP's list have seen one or more of these videos.

21 54% of the children whose parents have seen at least one video on the DPP's list have themselves seen at least one of these videos.

22 57% of the children whose parents have seen at least four videos on the DPP's list have seen one or more of these videos.

Acknowledgments

I would like to thank the National Society for the Prevention of Cruelty to Children for their co-operation in this study and in particular all the officers and families throughout the country who participated in the research. I would also like to thank Sue Creighton, Research Officer for the NSPCC, for all her help at every stage of the Enquiry.

Finally, I would like to thank Stephen Kay, MSc, MBCS, computer analyst at the University of Wales College of Medicine, Cardiff, who spent many hours helping me to analyse the statistics for this chapter.

6 Psychiatrists' Survey

Andrew Sims and Graham Melville-Thomas

The viewing of videos at home is necessarily, because of the recency of the technology, a new social phenomenon. We know little about the social characteristics of viewers, and almost nothing about long-term consequences. Two facts, however, are known beyond any contention: children and adolescents from the age of six or even younger are amongst the heaviest viewers; the level of violence portrayed and its explicitness is at times greater than that which would be tolerated by the British Board of Film Censors for an '18' rated film. This then is the starting point of our interest – that many very young children are watching videos and that these videos show violence of the most extreme kind.

There has been considerable work on the effects of violence shown on television upon both children and adults (see Chapter 2). The results of such studies are not easy to interpret, but Huesmann (1982) has summarised recent research: 'Violence viewing and aggressive behaviour clearly are positively related, not just in our culture but in other Western cultures as well. The weight of evidence strongly suggests that observational learning and attitude change induced by television violence are contributing to the positive relation.'

So far as violent viewing is concerned it is not possible in this survey to submit any conclusions regarding *the long-term effects* on minors in a representative way. For a study on the long-term effects of violent videos on children in British Society, a longer and cross-sectional sample is needed with the aid of a major child population statistical analysis; part of such a study should be prospective. Even with such a study and making allowance for the varied way in which child personality would affect the responses, it could prove difficult to separate the effects of violent video viewing from the effects of disturbing life events experienced by the child, notably violence within the home – parent to parent or parent to child; family threats and family breakdown.

At this relatively early stage of videos coming into British homes, we think it nevertheless important to gain a current impression of what is experienced in this way as reported by children and parents attending child psychiatric clinics.

Although there is doubt about the long-term consequences, the short-term effects of the portrayal of violence – the emotional experience of fear and excitement, horror and disgust – are the commercial reasons for the production of such material. There are many anecdotal accounts of these short-term reactions reaching extreme proportions. If the short-term effects of witnessing violence are so dramatic, what happens later on with persistent viewing of violence? Does the tolerance for the visual portrayal of violence increase so that the emotional response of excitement becomes less, and thus yet more intense stimulation is sought? Does the portrayal of fictional violence on the screen affect a person's attitudes to real violence? Does video violence stimulate individuals to take part in real acts of physical violence?

One theoretical notion that has been researched is the effect of emotional catharsis – put in simple terms: enabling a person to live a horrific experience in fantasy or imagination may prevent their having to act out such a happening in reality. The evidence is all against this concept – 'the available data convincingly contradict the catharsis model' (Huesman, 1982). Allowing violent individuals to experience vivid fantasy by the portrayal of violence does not reduce their level of actual physical violence.

There is, of course, enormous individual variation amongst people. Even if the response of a 'normal healthy' person subjected to the experience of video violence in their normal setting is of initial horror and excitement which quickly subsides, are there susceptible or vulnerable individuals for whom the consequences will be much more extreme? Children are generally thought to be more suggestible to what they witness on television than adults. Child and Adolescent Psychiatrists, in the course of their professional work see children who are emotionally and behaviourally disturbed. Such children are more likely both for social reasons to be heavy viewers of videos (more likely to come from socially isolated family units and more likely through inadequacy of social skills to spend time in solitary pursuits), and for psychological reasons to be more susceptible to the consequences of violence. Also psychiatrists regularly ask their patients about their emotional state and current behaviour, and the influences that have affected them currently. If there are short or long-term effects of video violence on children, this may therefore become apparent to Child and Adolescent Psychiatrists earlier than it would to other people, even parents and school teachers, and their opinion could therefore be relevant.

The report published in 1984 by the Parliamentary Group Video Enquiry – *Video Violence and Children: Children's Viewing Patterns and Parental Attitudes in England and Wales* – indicated that a considerable percentage of children had reported seeing one or more such violent videos (45% of children between the ages of 7 and 16 years). This chapter presents an investigation undertaken with the assistance of specialists in Child and

Adolescent Psychiatry (either consultants or senior registrars). From their responses, the aim is to find out if children and adolescents in a clinical setting give accounts of violent video viewing, and if so whether their symptoms are ever seen as associated with viewing videos.

Within medicine, scientific method has been applied to elicit the effect of a variable upon the state of health of the subject in the development of the *controlled clinical trial* (Doll, 1959). Essentially, this demands that a population should be randomly divided into two groups who are maintained in identical circumstances, except that one group is exposed to a known *influence* or treatment, and the other group is subjected to another influence, the effects of which are unknown. Neither the observer (researcher), nor the subject (patient), should know which type of influence any individual was exposed to until the completion of the trial: *double blind conditions*.

For complete scientific purity, the effects of video violence upon children would need to be investigated in this way. Because the effects of such an experiment could well be harmful to children, no researcher would carry out such a study and no Ethical Committee, for example, a District Health Authority, would pass such a project to be undertaken within its jurisdiction. As it is not possible to carry out research upon the effect of video violence directly, methods have to be devised for comparing those who have viewed videos with those who have not, and it is likely that there will be other confounding, socio-economic variables distinguishing between these two groups.

As the direct effects of video violence upon children cannot be measured, another way of gathering information is to enquire of relevant people concerning their observations. The professional opinion of those coming into contact with children, although, of course, subject to individual and collective prejudices, is worth ascertaining. A Child and Adolescent Psychiatrist (CAP) is trained to elicit the emotional state and psychological attitudes of young patients, to assess symptoms and evaluate the social and environmental situation of the individual. Training is also directed to ascertaining the effects of stress, changes in circumstances, recent life events and other current experiences upon the individual.

As the patients of the CAP may be considered to be abnormally vulnerable for the reasons given above, the psychiatrist is in a better position than a layman to give an opinion on whether video violence has any effect upon the patients he sees. If the opinion of most CAPs tends to point in the same direction, it then becomes a factor which should be given due weight in evaluating consequences. Opinion should not be confused with the observation of behaviour, but it can be sampled, surveyed and quantified to give valid and reliable findings (Oppenheim, 1968). The value of statements of opinion given by the majority of members of a complete cohort (all specialist CAPs in England and Wales) is much greater scientifically than anecdotal accounts from a few self-selected individuals.

The Content and Nature of the Violent Video

Some of the comments made by individuals following the recent press coverage of violent videos demonstrate a wide ignorance of the nature of the videotapes which are the concern of this report. For instance, they are not infrequently equated with the many stories, nursery rhymes, illustrations, films and other media which contain features of a dark, mysterious, threatening and even frightening nature. To equate the present violent videos with such stories is totally to misunderstand the basic *difference* between them. A clear distinction needs to be made, otherwise much confusion will result. Whereas the other type of material – whether in print or on the screen – is basically presented as fantasy, the so-called 'video nasties' show *real* people doing apparently *real* acts of sadistic violence and cruelty.

Hobgoblins and witches are as old as the hills, but the violent video is of a new and *different nature*. It portrays violence, sometimes mixed with sex, as committed by human adults often in realistic settings, for example a bedroom or the backstreets of a present-day city.

Many of the shots are taken from the point of view of the person committing the act. This could encourage an *identification of the viewer* with the perpetrator of the action. Such actions are slowly portrayed with a repeated dwelling on the violent, the macabre, and above all the sadistic. The message is clear; there is glorification of evil acts of violent and perverse nature. There is frequently no end point where the offender (the 'bad figure') is defeated and justice prevails – as is the universal theme of children's stories and rhymes and previous films and television programmes.

They do not portray the age-old confrontation of good versus evil, with the 'bad figures' eventually being overcome by the good – usually at the very end of the story. The standpoint of violent videos is quite the opposite. They show acts of violence and sadism as if they themselves could be carried out by the viewer. The settings are mostly present-day, though some have primitive settings of pre-history.

The content of violent videos is therefore likely to have a different effect upon all ages but especially the impressionable ages from childhood to young adulthood, and for this reason so much concern was felt by those responsible for promoting this investigation. While some children would laugh off these videos with a sense of bravado, the risk has to be faced that children could be affected by them in ways quite different from the reading or viewing of other children's (fantasy) material previously published.

The trend over the past decade for children to view films of an 'X' category (suitable only for viewers over 18) which increasingly portray sex with violence, is described in detail in *Video Violence: Children's Viewing Patterns and Parental Attitudes in England and Wales* (Hill *et al.*, 1984). Recently, children and adolescents have been exposed to videos, the central theme of which is the degrading of the human person in scenes of calculated violence.

Long before the arrival of the video recorder, films on sex and violence were screened in public cinemas, and some were viewed by minors. With the advent of the video recorder, however, films which could once only be seen at a cinema are now freely available on video. Examples of these are the films *Lemon Popsicle* and *Going Steady* (both from 1980), mentioned by children in *Children's Viewing Patterns and Parental Attitudes* as among 'their favourite and most remembered films'. Both of these are '18' or 'X' rated and by way of example the latter film was described by the Monthly Bulletin of the British Film Industry as 'an unremitting and hateful piece of exploitation, which takes the opportunity to abuse women in both script and shooting, with a sexism unknown to routine soft porn'.

The same kind of material is now being made on videotapes imported into this country and the accessibility to children is virtually uninvestigated. To compare such material with the content of children's fantasies and nursery rhymes is clearly inappropriate.

Availability to Children

Though the importation of videos with extreme and sadistic violence has been continuing for several years, it is only since early 1983 that the number and volume has increased so much and that they have become easily accessible to children and adolescents. For example the tapes are prominently displayed in many shops and petrol filling stations as well as in video clubs. There is only limited restriction on children or adolescents collecting them and viewing them at home.

Limitations in Assessment

Despite what has been said above, the actual knowledge of the content of such videos by personal viewing may be considered relatively limited *so far as professional persons* dealing with children are concerned. Many know about them only through press reports. No professional group has viewed them officially and given their initial impressions, simply because the material itself is considered illegal by the Director of Public Prosecutions, and once a title has been the subject of a successful prosecution or confiscation order, it tends to disappear from public display and is circulated more circumspectly. The one exception to this was when Members of Parliament were shown excerpts from some obscene video films during the debates on the Video Recordings Bill in 1984. The clips were compiled by Scotland Yard's Obscene Publications Department and some of the MPs were so disturbed by what they saw that they were unable to sit through the complete screening.

Aims and Method of this Study

The intention in circulating the questionnaires was to ascertain the opinion of practising, trained Child and Adolescent Psychiatrists concerning short-term effects of the new phenomenon of violent videos upon their patients. Those holding the post of consultant or senior registrar in the sub-speciality of Child and Adolescent Psychiatry within the National Health Service form the overwhelming majority of child psychiatrists in the United Kingdom, and see the vast majority of patients: almost all such doctors will be members (or fellows) of the Royal College of Psychiatrists. With a high response rate to the circulation of the questionnaire to all consultant and senior registrar CAPs, the survey can be said to represent the opinion of CAPs in Britain.

As violent videos are a new phenomenon, it was necessary to ask whether the psychiatrist normally made enquiry about viewing them. Opinion was sought on associations between videos and the patient's symptoms and behaviour, and whether such effects were generally beneficial or harmful. In order to achieve a rapid and completed response from most CAPs the questionnaire was severely curtailed in its detailed enquiry.

The *sample* of senior registrars and consultants in CAP was obtained from the computerised listing of the Section of Child and Adolescent Psychiatry of the Royal College of Psychiatrists. It is estimated that well over 95% of consultants and senior registrars in psychiatric specialties in the NHS are members of the Royal College of Psychiatrists, and all such CAP members will be members of the relevant Section. However, while there are 1048 members of the Section, there are known to be only 452 consultants and senior registrars in CAP in England and Wales (DHSS Statistics, 30 September 1983). Numbers of consultants and senior registrars for Scotland, Northern Ireland and the Irish Republic are not known. This study therefore maintains comparability with the rest of this book which concentrates upon England and Wales. There was no way of identifying those on the College list who were consultants and senior registrars in definitive posts short of circulation and enquiry, and this therefore had to be carried out for the whole Section. Exclusion was subsequently made therefore of:

1 Child psychiatrists who did not hold consultant or senior registrar posts;
2 Consultants and senior registrars whose posts were not within the definitive speciality of CAP;
3 CAPs from the Irish Republic, Scotland, and Northern Ireland;
4 Overseas members of the Section.

A postal survey was carried out initially of the complete Section whilst posting other notices, using the questionnaire regarding violent videos, shown on page 103. Non-respondents were subsequently re-circulated with a different covering letter. Respondents were asked if they would be prepared to collaborate in a further study and those from the first posting who agreed were asked for further information in a different questionnaire (shown on page 106).

Results of the Survey: 1 Questionnaire to all CAP Specialists

There are 1048 members of the Section of CAP of the Royal College of Psychiatrists, all of whom were circulated. There are known to be 452 consultants and senior registrars in CAP in England and Wales, the overwhelming majority of whom as members or fellows of the Royal College of Psychiatrists, would have been contacted. The total number of respondents who were consultants or senior registrars in CAP was 404, and of these 341 were working from addresses in England and Wales.

As we did not know how many specialist CAPs work in areas other than England and Wales, specialist CAPs in England and Wales only formed the target population and the response rate for this group was 75.4%. Of these 285 (83.6%) were consultants and 56 (16.4%) senior registrars. The majority of respondents in the target population spent their time in professional practice equally with adolescents and children, 203 (59.5%); 7 (2.1%) worked wholly with adolescents; 38 (11.1%) mostly with adolescents; 3 (0.9%) wholly with children; 54 (15.8%) mostly with children; and 34 (10.0%) had other distributions of working time.

Most respondents (211, 64.8%) had *occasionally* enquired whether their patients viewed violent videos; 21 respondents (6.2%) usually enquired whilst 97 (28.4%) never enquired.

One hundred and sixty-two (47.5%) respondents had received an account from at least one patient in the last year that a violent video had been influential on his or her emotional state or behaviour; one hundred and forty-five had received such accounts from less than 5 different patients, 14 from 5–10 patients, and 3 from more than 10 patients. One hundred and seventy-five respondents (51.3%) had never received any accounts from their patients that a violent video had been influential

One hundred and seventy-two (50.4%) respondents had thought there was an association between children's or adolescents' descriptions of their symptoms and their viewing violent videos; 149 of these had found an association in less than 5 patients, 19 in 5–10 patients, and 4 in more than 10 patients. One hundred and fifty respondents (44.0%) had never thought there was an association between their patients' symptoms and viewing violent videos.

Respondents were asked if the association they had found between the patients' symptoms and viewing violent videos, implied that symptoms had been precipitated or altered by viewing. Of those who had found an association (172 respondents), 62 (36.0%) thought that symptoms had on occasions been precipitated by violent videos, 62 (36.0%) thought that

Fig. 6.1 *Percentage of respondents who enquired whether their patients had ever viewed or viewed regularly violent videos*

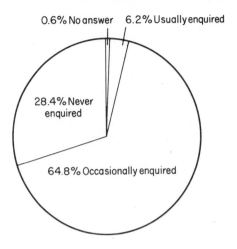

Fig. 6.2 *Percentage of respondents who had received an account from a parent/guardian that a violent video had been influential on his/her child's emotional state or behaviour*

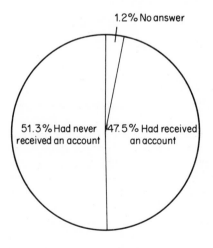

Fig. 6.3 *Percentage of respondents who had thought there was an association between children's or adolescents' descriptions of their symptoms and their viewing of violent videos*

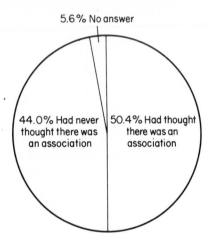

Fig. 6.4 *Percentage of respondents who thought that the effects, if any, on patients of viewing violent videos were either beneficial and reassuring or harmful and disturbing*

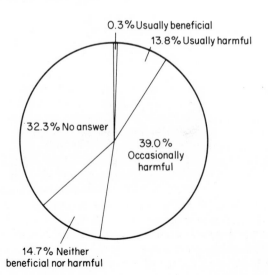

symptoms had not been thus precipitated, and a further 48 (27.9%) did not know or did not answer. Ninety-nine respondents (57.6%) considered that symptoms had been worsened by violent videos, none thought that symptoms had been ameliorated by watching and 16 (9.3%) thought that symptoms had been unchanged. Fifty-seven respondents (33.1%) did not know or did not answer.

When asked the general question, what, in their opinion, was the effect on patients of viewing violent videos?, one respondent (0.3%) considered them to be *usually* beneficial or reassuring, none considered them *occasionally* beneficial or reassuring, 47 (13.8%) thought they were *usually* harmful or disturbing, 133 (39.0%) found them *occasionally* harmful or disturbing, and 50 (14.7%) found them neither beneficial nor harmful. 110 (32.3%) did not know or did not answer or thought the answer was other than the choices given.

Respondents were asked if they had *ever* found a patient to show a reduction in violent behaviour following viewing violent videos (no association necessarily assumed). Four (1.2%) answered in the affirmative, but occasionally rather than frequently, while 240 (70.4%) answered negatively, and 97 (28.4%) did not know or did not answer.

Two hundred and seventy-seven respondents (81.2%) had considered violent videos to be a factor in children's and adolescents' lives before the survey, and 192 (56.3%) had held this view for more than a year before the survey.

Ninety-three respondents (27.3%) replied to the first posting, and 248 (72.7%) to the second. There were no significant differences between the answers of these two postings (Chi squared = 16.83; df = 25; p < 0.005).

The opinions of the respondents on whether violent videos are beneficial or harmful to those children or adolescents who watch them, varied greatly according to the respondents' answers to other questions. For example, 5.2% of those respondents who *never* enquired whether their patients viewed violent videos thought that watching violent videos was usually harmful and disturbing, while 16.3% of those respondents who *occasionally* enquired thought that watching violent videos was usually harmful or disturbing, and 28.6% of those who *usually* enquired thought that watching violent videos was usually harmful or disturbing.

Similarly, 14.4% of those who *never* enquired thought that violent videos can be occasionally harmful, while 49.8% of those who *occasionally* enquired and 42.9% of those who *usually* enquired thought that violent videos can be occasionally harmful. 52.9% of those who *never* enquired gave some other answer, did not know or did not answer the question on harmfulness; while only 20.4% of those who *occasionally* enquired, and 0.0% of those who *usually* enquired gave some other answer, did not know or did not answer. Those respondents who enquire about their patients' viewing habits are significant-

Fig. 6.5 *Percentage of respondents who thought that viewing violent videos was usually harmful or disturbing according to whether they enquired whether their patients viewed violent videos*

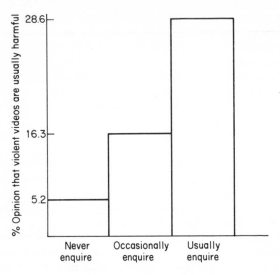

Fig. 6.6 *Percentage of respondents who held each opinion according to whether they had considered violent videos to be a factor in children's lives prior to the survey*

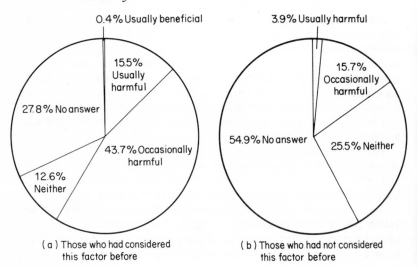

ly more likely to think violent videos are harmful than are those who don't enquire (Chi squared = 33.17; df = 1; p < 0.005).

Consideration of violent videos prior to this survey also significantly affected the respondents' opinions (Chi squared = 26.62; df = 1; p < 0.005). While 15.5% of those who *had* considered violent videos prior to this survey thought that watching violent videos is usually harmful, only 3.9% of those who *had not* held the same opinion. 43.7% of those who *had* considered it thought that violent videos could be occasionally harmful while only 15.7% of those who *had not* thought that they could be occasionally harmful. Only 12.6% of those who *had* considered violent videos prior to this survey thought that they were neither beneficial nor harmful while 25.5% of those who *had not* held the same opinion.

There were also some differences between consultants and senior registrars. Amongst consultants, 15.4% thought that violent videos were usually harmful, compared with only 5.4% of senior registrars. 38.2% of consultants and 42.9% of senior registrars thought violent videos were occasionally harmful. Therefore, consultants were significantly more likely than senior registrars to think that violent videos could be harmful or disturbing (Chi squared = 19.03; df = 1; p < 0.005).

Those respondents who have received an account about a violent video being influential on a patient's emotional state or behaviour are much more likely to hold the opinion that watching violent videos is harmful or disturbing than those who have not received any such account; 21.0% of those who had received at least one account thought that violent videos are usually harmful, while only 7.4% of those who had never received an account held the same opinion; 56.2% of those who had received an account thought that violent videos could be occasionally harmful while only 24.0% of those who had never received an account held this opinion. It also seems that those who have received at least one account about violent videos being influential on their patients' emotional state or behaviour are much less likely to hold a neutral opinion on violent videos (8.0%), than those respondents who have never received such an account (21.1%). The figures show that there is a significant difference between the opinions of those who have received accounts about violent videos being influential on children's emotional state and behaviour, and the opinions of those who have never received such accounts (Chi squared = 27.26; df = 1; p < 0.005).

There is similarly a significant difference between the opinions of those who have found at least one association between their patients' symptoms and their viewing violent videos and the opinions of those respondents who have never found an association (Chi squared = 37.05; df = 1; p < 0.005). 22.7% of those who have found at least one association think that watching violent videos is usually harmful compared with only 2.7% of those who have never found an association. 56.4% of those who have found an association believe that violent videos are occasionally harmful while only 23.3% of those who have never found such an association hold this opinion. Those who have found at least one association are much less likely to be neutral than those who have not: 7.6% of those who have found an association thought that violent videos were neither beneficial nor harmful and 12.8% of these respondents did not know or did not answer; while 24.7% of those who had never found an association believed that violent videos were neither beneficial nor harmful and 49.3% did not know or did not answer.

It seems therefore that those respondents who have *received accounts*, or have *found associations* are much more likely to believe that watching violent videos is harmful. However, the results also show that those respondents who enquired about their patients' viewing habits are much more likely to have received accounts or found associations. For example, only 16.5% of those respondents who had *never* enquired whether their patients viewed violent videos had received at least one account about violent videos being influential on the patient's emotional state or behaviour, while 57.9% of those who *occasionally* enquired and 85.7% of those who *usually* enquired had received at least one account. Similarly, only 21.7% of those respondents who *never* enquired had found at least one association, while 60.7% of those who *occasionally* enquired and 80.9% of those who *usually* enquired had found at least one association.

We must therefore conclude that **the number of accounts a respondent has received, and the number of associations a respondent has found, are significantly affected by whether that respondent enquires into his patients' viewing habits or not** (Chi squared = 32.41; df = 1; p < 0.005 and Chi squared = 26.76; df = 1; p < 0.005 respectively).

Out of the 151 respondents who had enquired whether their patients viewed violent videos, *and* had found associations between their patients' symptoms and their viewing violent videos, 1 respondent (0.7%) thought that violent videos were usually beneficial or reassuring; 0 respondents (0.0%) thought that they were occasionally beneficial or reassuring; 36 respondents (23.8%) thought that violent videos were usually harmful or disturbing; 90 respondents (59.6%) thought that they were occasionally harmful or disturbing; 11 respondents (7.3%) thought that they were neither beneficial nor harmful; and 13 respondents (8.6%) did not know or did not answer.

Out of the 180 respondents who thought that violent videos were usually or occasionally harmful or disturbing, 120 respondents (66.7%) had enquired *and* received accounts; 126 respondents (70%) had enquired *and* thought there was an association; and 113 respondents (62.8%) had received accounts *and* found associations.

There was only one respondent who considered that the effect on patients of viewing violent videos had been beneficial and reassuring, and this person thought that it was *usually* rather than *occasionally* beneficial on the evidence of no cases. Further enquiry was made by telephone of this person who was a

Fig. 6.7   *Percentage of respondents who held each opinion according to whether they had received any accounts about a violent video being influential on a child's emotional state or behaviour*

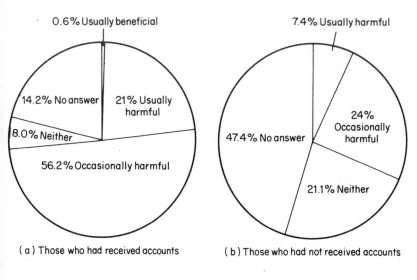

(a) Those who had received accounts   (b) Those who had not received accounts

Fig. 6.8   *Percentage of respondents who held each opinion according to whether they had found any associations between their patients' viewing patterns and their symptoms*

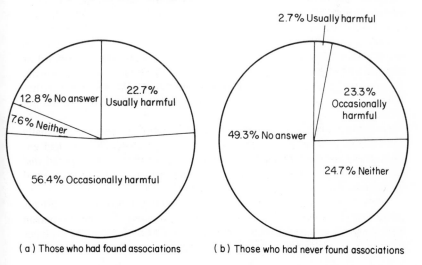

(a) Those who had found associations   (b) Those who had never found associations

senior registrar whose basic medical training had been overseas. Despite receiving the documents in the Appendix (including the definition and examples of violent videos), the respondent had not realised that the questionnaire referred to the degree of violence as defined under *violent videos* but thought that the Enquiry referred to everyday television programmes. With regard to violent videos, the respondent was of the opinion that 'such things do affect those who are vulnerable and cannot have any good effect upon people'.

Discussion

This survey of the opinion of consultant and senior registrar CAPs can reasonably be claimed to be representative of psychiatrists dealing with young people in England and Wales. Five-sixths of the sample were in the more senior grade of Consultant Psychiatrist. Like the ECT survey for general adult psychiatry (Pippard and Ellam, 1981), this survey taps the experience and opinion of psychiatrists in a comprehensive manner only possible in Britain through the good offices of the Royal College of Psychiatrists.

More than half this population work approximately equally with adolescents and younger children; just under one-sixth work predominantly with younger children, and about 10% predominantly with adolescents. There are a few psychiatrists working in a different way, for example, exclusively with whole families.

Contrary to the expectations of many senior CAPs themselves and of the research team, a very large majority of respondents were already aware of *violent videos* as a factor in the lives of the children whom they treated prior to the survey, with more than half aware for longer than a year. This was striking, as the violent video material which is the subject of this Enquiry (definition contained in Appendix 1) had only been available for about 18 months–2 years in the United Kingdom at the time of the survey. More than two-thirds of respondents were already making enquiries as to whether their patients viewed violent videos, and half of the patients responded to this question in the affirmative. Thus the hypothesis that the patients of CAPs were very likely also to be viewers of violent videos, was substantiated.

About half of the respondents had received accounts indicating that violent videos were influential on the patient's emotional state or behaviour, and a similar proportion thought that there was an association between their patients' symptoms and their viewing patterns. More than half the respondents believed that viewing was at least occasionally harmful or disturbing for their patients; 15% considered them to be neutral.

When only those respondents who enquire about their patients' viewing patterns are considered, the figures for potentially harmful effects become higher: 60.3% give an account about violent videos being influential upon a patient's emotional state or behaviour; 62.3% had found an association between a patient's description of their symptoms and viewing; 66.5% thought that viewing violent videos could be harmful or disturbing. Those respondents who did not enquire about viewing violent videos were less likely to believe that videos were harmful; this presumably being at least one of the reasons why they did not enquire into this area of their patients' lives.

Of those respondents who had received an account of a violent video being influential on a patient's emotional state or behaviour, 77.2% believed that viewing violent videos could be harmful or disturbing, and 79.1% of those respondents who had found an association between their patients' symptoms and viewing violent videos believed that viewing violent videos could be harmful or disturbing.

Thus the more psychiatrists know about the content of violent videos and the viewing habits of their patients, the more likely they are to believe that they may be a potent and harmful influence upon their patients; when they enquire of their patients' viewing, they find that there is sometimes an association between watching and the patient's emotional state, behaviour or symptoms. **Most respondents believed that, in their experience or opinion, the effect of viewing violent videos was at least occasionally harmful or disturbing,** and this percentage increased amongst those who enquired about violent videos, and yet more amongst those who had received an account of an association between viewing and the patient's mental state, behaviour or symptoms.

In summary, we may conclude that the more information CAPs had in this area, the more convinced they were that violent videos were potentially harmful to their patients. The only psychiatrist who thought that viewing could be beneficial on any occasion had misunderstood the term *violent video*.

Further Enquiry of Collaborators

One hundred and twenty-six respondents volunteered to participate in further research. However only those volunteers who responded to the first posting were enquired of further; they were asked to complete the questionnaire shown on page 106 (Questionnaire for Respondents: Violent Video Enquiry) for each of a prospective series of 10 consecutive patients.

Total number of respondents = 11
Total number of patients   = 98

1 Twenty-three (23.5%) patients had watched violent videos.
2 Nine (39%) patients who had watched violent videos had been influenced in their emotional state or behaviour.
3 In five (21.7%) patients who had watched violent videos, there was considered to be an association between the patients' description of symptoms and viewing.

4 In one case symptoms were thought to have been precipitated by videos.
5 In three cases existing symptoms were considered to have been made
   worse by viewing violent videos; in 17 cases symptoms were unchanged
   and in no cases were symptoms ameliorated.
6 In the psychiatrists' opinions for seven cases the effect of viewing violent
   videos was at least occasionally harmful or disturbing; in 18 cases viewing
   was neutral and in no cases beneficial.

Summary

Four hundred and four consultants and senior registrars, working within the
field of Child and Adolescent Psychiatry were asked their opinion by
questionnaire concerning the effects of violent videos upon their patients.
Three hundred and forty-one (75.4%) of those resident in England and
Wales completed and returned the questionnaire; 81.2% of respondents had
considered that video was a significant factor in their patients' lives prior to
the survey (56.3% more than a year previously). 71.0% of respondents
inquired whether their patients viewed violent videos. 46.6% of respondents
had received an account that a violent video had been influential on a
patient's emotional state or behaviour.

50.5% of respondents had thought that there was an association between
their patients' symptoms and their viewing violent videos; 52.8% of respondents believed that, in their experience and opinion, the effect of viewing
violent videos was at least occasionally harmful or disturbing. 66.1% of child
psychiatrists who enquired about their patients' viewing believed violent
videos to be at least occasionally harmful; of those psychiatrists who had
received an account *and* had found an association between viewing and their
patients' mental state, behaviour and symptoms, 83.7% believed violent
videos to be harmful.

Further information was obtained from 98 patients of 11 CAPs. One
quarter of these patients had watched violent videos. Of those who had
watched, two-fifths had been influenced by them; in one-fifth symptoms
were associated with viewing; in some cases symptoms were precipitated or
exacerbated by viewing. 28% of those watching were considered to have
experienced a disturbing or harmful effect and in no case were violent videos
beneficial.

The significance of making enquiry of Child and Adolescent Psychiatrists
was that such psychiatrists normally ask detailed questions about the
influences upon the life of the children in their care; they are more likely to
see older children and adolescents than infants and younger children; the
patients they see are likely to be especially vulnerable for psychological and
social reasons to any potentially harmful influence. The 75% of all the Child
and Adolescent Psychiatrists in England and Wales who responded forming

our sample gave a remarkably unanimous opinion that violent videos were frequently associated with the patients' symptoms in a deleterious manner and that this material was generally harmful in its effects upon the children they saw.

Acknowledgments

We would like to thank all the consultant psychiatrists and senior registrars, Fellows and Members of the Child and Adolescent Section of the Royal College of Psychiatrists for their co-operation with this study. We also wish to thank Miss Jane Boyce for organising the posting of the questionnaire and Miss Alison Hill for statistical work. We are also most grateful to the staff in the Computer Department of the University of Wales College of Medicine, Cardiff for their valuable contribution in the analysis of statistical data.

References

DOLL, R. (1959) in WITTS, L. J. (ed.) *Medical Surveys & Clinical Trials*. London: Oxford University Press.

HILL, C., DAVIS, H., HOLMAN, R. and NELSON, G. (1984) *Video Violence and Children: Children's Viewing Patterns and Parental Attitudes in England and Wales*. London: Parliamentary Group Video Enquiry.

HUESMANN, L. R. (1982) 'Television violence and aggressive behaviour', in PEARL, D., BOUTHILET, L. and LAZAR, J. *Television and Behaviour*. US Department of Health and Human Services, Rockville.

OPPENHEIM, A. N. (1966) Design and Attitude Measurement (Questionnaire). London: Heinemann

PIPPARD, J. and ELLAM, L. (1981) *Electroconvulsive Treatment in Great Britain*. London: Gaskell.

Questionnaires

Appraisal of Consultant and Senior Registrars in Child and Adolescent Psychiatry on Their Opinion Concerning the Effects of Violent Videos upon Their Patients

Name ....

In the following questionnaire please circle the number next to your answer.

If you would like to supply additional comments or empirical evidence/examples from your practice that will be of assistance in this research please write them on other sheets of paper and attach them to this questionnaire.

1   Are you a consultant in child and/or adolescent psychiatry?   1
    a senior registrar in child and/or adolescent psychiatry   2
    a consultant paediatrician   3
    a senior registrar paediatrician   4
    a child health consultant   5
    a child health registrar   6
    Other (please specify)   7
    ....

2   How would you describe the time you spend in professional practice?
    Wholly with adolescents (13+)   1
    Mostly with adolescents (13+)   2
    Wholly with children   3
    Mostly with children   4
    Equally with adolescents and children   5
    Other (please specify)   6
    ....

3   Have you enquired whether your patients have ever viewed, or view regularly,
    violent videos?
    never   1
    occasionally   2
    usually   3

4   In the last year have you received any accounts from a patient about a violent
    video being influential on his/her emotional state or behaviour?
    never   1
    less than 5 different patients   2
    5–10 patients   3
    more than 10 patients   4
    If you have could you give brief details below
    ....
    ....
    ....

5   Have you thought there was ANY association between children's or adolescents'
    description of their symptoms and their viewing violent videos?
    never   1
    less than 5 different patients   2
    5–10 patients   3
    more than 10 patients   4
    If you have could you give brief details below
    ....
    ....
    ....

    if so,
    a) did you think symptoms were precipitated by videos?
            Yes   1
            No   2
            Don't know   3

b) did you think existing symptoms were altered by violent videos?

symptoms worsened 1
symptoms ameliorated 2
symptoms unchanged 3
don't know 4

6 In your opinion, from your experience, has the effect on patients of viewing violent videos been

usually beneficial or reassuring 1
occasionally beneficial or reassuring 2
usually harmful or disturbing 3
occasionally harmful or disturbing 4
neither beneficial nor harmful 5
Other (please specify) 6
....

7 Have you ever found a patient who has shown a reduction in violent behaviour following viewing violent videos?

Yes 1
No 2
Don't know 3

If yes
frequently 1
occasionally 2

8 Due to the fact that the video is a recent phenomenon in Britain many professional people have not been aware of it being a factor in children's and adolescents' lives. Had you considered it prior to this survey?

Yes 1
No 2
Don't know 3

9 If you answered 'yes' to question 8 could you give some indication of how long ago you became aware of this.

more than a week ago 1
more than a month ago 2
more than 3 months ago 3
more than 6 months ago 4
more than a year ago 5

10 Would you be prepared to participate in a further piece of research with guided questionnaires to selected patients or their parents? Would you please indicate below and we will send you the relevant paper. Your local ethical committee must be consulted.

Yes 1
No 2
Don't know 3

Questionnaire for Respondents: Violent Video Enquiry

Patient No ....

Please circle appropriate response

1 Has the patient watched violent videos?
    No 1
    Yes 2
    Not enquired 3

2 In the last year has a violent video been influential in his/her emotional state or behaviour?
    not at all 1
    possibly 2
    probably 3
    definitely 4

   Could you give brief details:

3 Do you think there has been any association between the patient's description of symptoms and viewing violent videos?
    not at all 1
    possibly 2
    probably 3
    definitely 4

4 Do you think symptoms were precipitated by videos?
    No 1
    Yes 2
    Don't know 3

5 Do you think that existing symptoms were altered by viewing violent videos?
    symptoms: worse 1
                  ameliorated 2
                  unchanged 3
                  don't know 4

6 In your opinion, has the effect on this patient of viewing violent videos been:
    usually beneficial or reassuring 1
    occasionally beneficial or reassuring 2
    occasionally harmful or disturbing 3
    usually harmful or disturbing 4
    neither beneficial nor harmful 5

Please comment further if appropriate:

Date : _____

7 Psychiatrists' Case Studies – The Nature of Effects on Children and Adolescents

Graham Melville-Thomas and Andrew Sims

The preceding chapter has given an overview of the opinions of professional Child and Adolescent Psychiatrists. We now turn to consider the nature of the effects on children seen in clinical situations. This has been done through a compilation of the individual reports given to us in brief case descriptions by professionals dealing with children and adolescents.

For purposes of confidentiality the cases themselves are described in such a way that anonymity is ensured. In order to obtain some idea of the nature of the immediate effects on some children and adolescents, information from the case studies has been abstracted so as to indicate the overall patterns of reaction in children referred. It has to be made clear at the outset that the children and adolescents reported had been referred to clinics, and as such do not represent a typical cross section of the child community. However, many more children with similar reactions and disturbances are likely to be found in the community without any referral to clinics. The data obtained was from children and parents who chose to seek help, either directly because of a disturbance following violent video viewing, or because of some other general problem such as disturbed behaviour, sleep difficulties, or problems of nervousness or educational adjustment. In the second category, associations with videos emerged by chance during the interviews.

Considering the recency of the impact of the extremely violent videotapes, we have been surprised at the number of cases reported as being disturbed by such viewing. The age range of the children who have been found to be affected by viewing violent videos has also been wider than expected, from pre-school through to adolescence. The reports, however, are not large in number and are not considered by us as in any way representative or statistically based. Nevertheless, we consider them of sufficiently important *descriptive value* to give a clear indication of how some children will react to scenes of violence. The effects fall into seven categories, namely:

1 Anxiety symptoms   2 Sleep disturbances
3 Depression with phobia   4 Behaviour disorders
5 Over-excitement   6 Distortion of reality
7 Psychosis – precipitated or worsened

1 Anxiety symptoms

The recent literature contains only one case report of a young person suffering an anxiety state considered to have been precipitated by the viewing of a horror film (Mathai, 1983). However, a small number of case reports appeared about ten years ago following such films as *The Exorcist* (Bozzuto, 1975) but these concerned young adults. The reports given to us through the survey provide descriptions of comparable anxiety reactions in children. For example, a nine-year-old temperamentally anxious girl who had disturbing early experiences was precipitated into an acute anxiety state by a violent video.

Many other reports have been received of children under ten-years-old suffering strong daytime anxiety accompanied by night terrors. One professional experience was of sudden symptoms of anxiety usually starting after the child had viewed a violent video film with a friend. The children presenting these symptoms had never viewed violent videos before, and although on enquiry they were of anxious disposition, they had never needed treatment previously. One boy, fearful of going to bed, was visibly nervous and could hardly leave his mother's side between the time of viewing a particular horror video and his referral to a clinic. As in other similar cases, the boy's mother had at once noticed her son's strong avoidance reaction by closing his eyes when viewing the tape. Persistent, tearful episodes followed that evening. According to the information given to us, reactions of this sort and in varying degree can and do follow after children have viewed horror videos.

Anxiety symptoms are characteristically of a sudden onset following the viewing of violent video material and indicate that the child is struggling to come to terms with the onrush of violent and sadistic material not previously experienced. In some cases there was a re-enacting by the child with verbal and physical recall of the most disturbing part of the tape. Some children were already of anxious disposition, but did not have the overt symptoms until after the video.

The case accounts we received gave a wide variation in response to violent videos. A few more tough-minded children were inclined to report the videos as exciting and 'OK', or even 'good'. On further questioning however even tough-minded adolescents were known to admit they would not wish to see the tapes again and would not like to expose others, especially younger children to them. This mature response is encouraging, and was expressed in statements such as: 'No, I would not like others, especially younger children, to see such things – it would not be right, it would not be good for them.'

We have had accounts giving us an understanding of how some children seek to cope with frightening videotapes. The reactions strongly resemble those in younger children looking at fantasy films on television. For example, a child typically closes his eyes or retreats behind a piece of furniture but only a few leave the room.

The difference between a child watching fantasy films on television and this new form of violent video is the extent of the reaction which follows. Many children after the younger years recognise the fantasy nature of much that is on television, but the violent videos are so realistic as to have a direct impact.

Examples were given when the child was thought by the parents not to have been watching because he had turned away or closed his eyes. Subsequent reactions in the child sometimes surprised the parents, who had underestimated the impact of even a short scene watched. Such reactions can be strong and immediate, and as previously quoted going to bed or separating from the mother sometimes became acutely difficult. Depending on the handling of the situation by the parent, the child's personality, and other factors, this acute phobia either diminished or persisted. Sometimes the parents noted a repetition in play of a video scene. Sometimes sleep problems persisted.

The patterns are various and the outcome depends on many factors other than the video itself. Much may depend on how the parent deals with the reaction. That it is a clearly and directly associated fear phenomenon of a degree stronger than anything else previously experienced by children and adolescents is evident already from what has been observed and reported to us by those who took part in our survey.

The response of children and adults to varying degrees of violence in television and films, have been carefully monitored in a wide series of investigations (see References on page 22). It would be ethically improper as well as unlawful to expose children to violent videos, since the content of these films is so much more potentially disturbing. Their nature is of a different order. The growth of screen violence over past years has now resulted in the so-called 'video nasties'. The effects of continued future exposure to such tapes can only be conjectured against this preliminary background of reported case findings where children were found to have been behaviourally or emotionally affected.

The general impact as a learning process must surely be wider. Carruthers and Taggart (1973) at the end of a scientifically detailed study of physiological responses to violent films and television refer to this in their paper: 'Much research already carried out (Halloran, 1967; Hamburg, 1971) has consistently shown that violent behaviour can be learnt from films and television.

Like most teaching it is especially effective at an early age when related to real life situations, carried out by people with whom the subject can identify, made interesting and exciting and, above all, when it is rewarded and encouraged by peer groups.'

2 Sleep disturbances

These are considered in a separate category because they indicated such a relatively common way for an anxiety reaction in the child to be expressed. Symptoms varied from insomnia to nightmares, sleep walking and night terrors. One doctor reported seeing three or four children who had sleep disturbances clearly attributed to video watching. In this series of cases there was either straightforward sleep disturbance with no daytime expression, or cases in which the children imitated the extreme form of violence or horror which most impressed them. In some cases, anxiety persisted alone, in others aggressive behaviour followed.

We have had reports of children with disturbed sleep and nightmares with various phobic disorders including school phobia. In each case viewing of a particular video could be traced. One case described a boy of only four-years-old who began to suffer sleeplessness and night terrors after watching a violent video. Any idea that children of this age are too young to react to video violence is dispelled by this and similar cases.

Seven- and eight-year-old children are also very impressionable as indi-cated by one child in this age group who was fascinated by violent videos. One girl exposed to a lot of horror video was pre-occupied with blood and murder, death and violence, but in her case no sleep disturbances were noted. Another child of this same age range expressed fascination at first but also had violent dreams and exhibited aggressive behaviour towards other children.

It is not clear at this time to what extent children are less likely to have sleep disorders if they are able to imitate, act out, or in other ways express what they have seen that disturbs them. What has emerged from the cases described to us is that a varied pattern exists and seems to be present throughout childhood.

3 Depression and phobic reactions

These were emotional disorders in two children. There was a depressive and phobic response in a child of low average intelligence who also had sleep difficulties, while a twelve-year-old child became depressed with obsessional symptoms and a fear of returning to school.

4 Behaviour disorders

This amounted to sufficient acute disturbance of behaviour over and above any previous response which the child had exhibited. By definition the response was sufficient for the parents to seek specialist professional help and advice. Some children were described as preoccupied with aggression and violence and for some this was more general in nature. More commonly it was clear from the parents and children that the behaviour was a *close reflection* of the violent scenes in the video. For example, an act of violence toward another child, not necessarily from the same family, could be copied from a violent act on the video.

Confirmation of the behaviour stemming from a video was possible in cases where the parents had also seen the same video. In a few instances a child has carried out definite acts of considerable, and sometimes serious, aggression leading to injury. Sometimes this injury was inflicted on another child, sometimes on a domestic animal.

The behavioural affects which were reported to us fall into three categories:
(a) Imitative
(b) Sexual
(c) Aggressive

Imitative behaviour
Cases were described where it was clear that the wayward behaviour by a child was a direct copying of what had been seen on the video. A small group of children developed disturbed and bizarre ideas relating to the occult and violence after viewing this type of video, with a resulting alleged attempt to drown another child. One report informed us of a boy responding to a television programme and when asked why he had taken an overdose of tablets, he said 'that is what depressed people do'. He was presumably depressed at the time and had seen an overdosing sequence on film. One girl was strongly influenced by a 'video nasty' in which very realistic combinations of sex and violence were portrayed. This led to the embroidering of sexual fantasies about real people.

Sexual/aggressive behaviour
With the considerable combination of realistically portrayed violence with sex in several of the obscene videos, it is not surprising that several accounts were received of wayward sexual behaviour following some viewings. One young adolescent assaulted a young girl within 24 hours of watching a gang rape on such a video. Almost certainly the same video, *I Spit on Your Grave*, was the precursor to a gang rape of a schoolgirl. There was a clear association with a scene in the video programme.

Aggressive behaviour
This was relatively common in the cases reported but several psychiatrists

also noted previous (ie pre-viewing) tendencies to aggression. A few children had clearly experienced overt aggression if not violence mainly between their parents.

One boy repeated in his play a particular video scene. He had nightmares after watching the video and launched an attack on his brother. Even after recall and description of a video in detail there is no guarantee of the impulsive arousal being dissipated. This is indicated in a few cases. In one case a boy described a strangling scene in a group story telling, but was later found attempting to choke another child.

One or two instances occurred among the mentally handicapped. A violent and pornographic video was watched at home by children with a mentally handicapped man who later indecently assaulted them.

One family arranged parties with the showing of violent and pornographic videos. These were 'understood' by one child in the family to increase the general pattern of family interaction.

One doctor was impressed by the extent to which he found daytime viewing of videos in unemployed families when he made visits to their homes. Another child, just starting school, was sadistic to a pet following the viewing of a violent video and one adolescent described sexual fantasies of a sadistic nature which he did not have before viewing a particular video. Though not acted upon in this last case, other adolescents were reported as occasionally acting out these newly learned aggressive/sadistic behaviours.

In a few cases, aggressive/sadistic crimes were mentioned without details. There were three cases in which actual bodily harm had been inflicted. One of these involved a ten-year-old boy subject to severe rages who, on one occasion, had injured a teacher by stabbing her. He subsequently attacked and stabbed another child and gave an account revealing that a couple of days earlier he had seen a thriller video at home in which a murderer had killed someone with a knife. The boy's mother said he had copied the behaviour from the film. He was a boy frustrated by learning difficulties and reactions from other pupils and he suffered several frustrations and tensions at home. The video seemed to play a contributory part.

Another disturbed boy of 15-years-old who was at a special residential establishment had previously committed minor offences. During a visit home one weekend he watched a film on television in which a woman was stabbed while in the shower. On the way back to the school he broke into a house which he tried to set on fire. Later, on reaching the school, he entered one of the staff houses and stabbed the wife of a member of staff while she was in bed. The psychiatrist thought that this boy had been directly influenced in his actions by the film.

While these instances so far reported are few, the evidence that such direct copying by children can occur as a result of violent video viewing is a serious indicator of what might happen should a freer access to such material be allowed. Short of actual damaging behaviour, aggressive responses occurred in other ways. For instance, a child might identify with the perpetrator of the violence and express this either verbally or in play acting on his own or with other children.

Forms of violent behaviour, previously unknown, were soon adopted by children in their play when these were seen on television or video. This is a well-known phenomenon and since play is the child's natural and healthy mode of expression, especially in younger years, it is not surprising to have reports of 'video' behaviour brought out in play therapy.

Evidence, therefore, is accumulating that a new dimension of violence is being acted out in play at all ages, and this evidently has a direct basis in the '18' rated video, the nature of which was not previously accessible to children. These films were previously available only in the cinema with the safeguard of the '18' certification. Both teachers and child psychiatrists have reported this phenomenon in play whether or not the particular child is also acting out aggressive behaviour.

The copying effect is most seriously seen in actual repetition of violent acts shown on the video, for example, sadistic murder or rape. So far, very few cases have been reported and these have been almost entirely in adults. The case of cannabilistic murder committed in West Germany in 1984, where the crime mimicked the content of a violent video is a good example. Clearly there is a greater risk of identification and copying in individuals who already show tendencies towards instability and poor impulse control, and this was borne out by the information given to us.

5 Over-excitement

Parents, particularly fathers, obtained the violent videos which the children found exciting but not 'abnormal'. Problems of control of aggression and anxiety were made worse by viewing such material according to one psychiatrist though cause and effect relationships were hard to establish.

In more than one instance the child 'blamed' the video for his actions. One teenage boy said the programme had caused him to have disturbed behaviour through its stimulating effects. With all such accounts it is fairly clear that other factors have had profound effects upon the child, but the recent wave of videos has added its own weight in exciting children into wayward and often aggressive or violent actions which both the adolescents and the parents attribute partly to the videos.

Younger children gave a straightforward but often detailed account of videos when questioned, as in the case of the nine-year-old boy who was pre-occupied with his own badness and the devil on account of his behaviour towards his peers. Aggravation of the symptoms by violent videos was noted by the specialist.

6 *Distortion of reality*

There were a couple of instances in which the child was not seriously disturbed but had developed ideas about sexual behaviour and violence in other ordinary human beings which were clearly exaggerated or totally opposed to reality. Though television has been researched, it is quite impossible at this stage even to guess at the extent to which children and teenagers may have become additionally or unrealistically anxious about being abused or exploited. Some of our contributors raised questions about this issue, and one referred to discussions which have taken place at Child Abuse Congresses in recent years.

7 *Psychosis*

Psychosis is the most severe of psychiatric disorders which may occur in adolescents, to a lesser extent in children, and has an unknown and probably complex aetiology. One case was noted where a 13-year-old developed a transient psychosis shortly after watching a horror video. The stimulant effect upon primitive urges in the unstable young person was commented upon by another psychiatrist. It seems, therefore, potentially likely that very unstable individuals will be adversely affected. Out of our small sample we were in fact surprised to have two cases quoted. One of these was of a psychotic adolescent who was reported to have become severely disturbed immediately after viewing a violent video with his peer group. Psychotic hallucinations were probably related to the film seen.

Other comments

Finally, there were several references to general aspects of video viewing and the family but without actual symptom association in children. For example, several found that parents usually substantiated what their children had independently said about videos. The 'no warnings given' invitation to a party where a horror video was shown has caused distress amongst parents. Some children were frightened, others excessively fascinated, morbidly dwelling on the subject of the videotape. In at least one area reactions were sufficient for the local school to be alerted. Presumably the video parties stopped.

This brings us to our final observation, namely, that after the parents have been advised to stop showing violent videos, the behaviour improves. These comments, views and descriptions of professional colleagues have mainly pointed in one common direction namely that violent videos or films *may have* disturbing effects upon some of the children referred to them. The degrees and variety of reaction are considerable and cover a wider range than we had earlier anticipated.

Personality Variables

Children and adolescents vary greatly in personality and therefore in response but are generally more suggestible than adults. The older adolescents who are already preoccupied with violence from a disturbed background and who have poor impulse control are made particularly vulnerable by repeated stimulation from violent scenes portrayed in videotapes which are so easily hired and viewed at leisure. Such individuals are often isolated and carry out crimes of violence on their own.

Some adolescents were reported to have group video viewings which would be followed by asocial acts of crime which were not directly related to the content of the video. Acts of delinquency following such group viewing, were destruction of property, burglary or similar acts of wanton behaviour. In such cases what happened was of a general nature, not a repetition of what had been seen on tape hours earlier.

In some reported instances, therefore, there was a collective response associated with a lowering of moral behavioural standards. There is also evidence of instances when adolescents who play truant meet in a home during the day when the parents are at work; a video is watched and they then commit a crime of a general nature, ie not specifically related to the video content.

The type of videotape we are concerned with is still relatively little known first hand by the public at large. The essence of it is to portray acts of violence against the person (or animal) and to present this not only realistically but in such a way that it is condoned. There is no end point of the criminal being detected let alone caught or punished; and it could be the general denials of justice, retribution, or goodness implicit in so many of these videos that triggers an act of delinquency whether alone or in a group.

There is usually no real story in these video films and no account of recovery, much less a correcting or hero type who puts things right at the end. The aim appears to be one of repeatedly stressing the emotionally sick and perverted behaviour theme, so as to have this play upon the mind of the viewer. It is not surprising therefore that accounts varied. There were those who found the tapes shocking, revulsive, and these young persons or children said they would not wish to view them again. On the other hand, there were some who said they enjoyed the tapes, and one boy was mentioned as having mainly sadistic interest in the tapes.

With regard to the variation in personality, previously stressed by Eysenck and Nias, several commentators made the point that in terms of mixed behavioural/anxiety reactions, the children with existing personality problems were often more affected. In a similar way children with past or present tendencies to weaker impulse control and aggression were found to be most influenced to behave in an aggressive or destructive manner.

Fright Responses in Children

Quite apart from the actual overt childhood disturbances emerging after video watching, many children experience emotional responses to potentially frightening material on the mass media and in the cinema (Eisenberg, 1936; Preston, 1941; Wertham, 1953; Himmelweit, Oppenheim and Vince, 1958).

Previous investigators provide some insight into the way children react emotionally to such experiences. As Professor J. Cantor (1982) has indicated, there has been a falling off in concern about the effects of the mass media on the young after an earlier focus on this subject 20–40 years ago. She has indicated how little has been written about this over the intervening years – a period when both cinema and television have become an increasing part of the daily life experience of children, and when the horror content has steadily risen. She quotes Singer as 'a notable exception to this lack of interest', and as someone describing the possible long-lasting effects in children's minds of fright experiences as a result of horror films on television or in the cinema. Singer expressed concern that exposure of children to films which contained scenes sufficiently frightening to be beyond their capacity to tolerate or accept, could result in persistent night terrors and weird fantasies, lasting for years. If this is so for films, the potential of this outcome from video nasties for some children would be even greater.

The effects upon children will obviously vary according to several factors.

1 Development

The first of these is the developmental stage the child has reached at the time of viewing. Three- to four-year-old children were found to respond quite differently from nine- to ten-year-olds in one study (Cantor, 1982). Parents were asked to complete a questionnaire which included their observations on which of a series of programmes caused a fright in their child. Only about a third of parents responded. The television programmes included *The Incredible Hulk, The Wizard of Oz*, television news, *Halloween, Little House on the Prairie* and others of similar nature.

The more grotesque and fantastic characters frightened the younger children more than the older group. The more *realism* entered into the films, the more the *older child group* became affected emotionally with fright responses.

This study underlines the distinction that has to be made between fantasy material and realistic material on the media because of the increasing effect of the latter upon older children. Carrying this consideration into the realm of the violent video, it would be logical to assume an even greater frightening and disturbing effect from the violent videos, because of their harsh and extreme realism. This often creates the illusion of involving the viewer. The camera in some violent videos is placed not in the position of the observer but in the place of the victim or the perpetrator of the violence. One such example is a film that puts the viewer in the position of a couple being axed by a boy enraged by his parent's act of infidelity. Such realism is extreme and is in stark contrast to both fantasy films and to 'ordinary' horror films where the viewer is always an onlooker.

2 Personality

The second factor of variability is the personality of the child. There do appear to be some who seem to relish the macabre or the violent. Such children will repeatedly view videos with a search for greater and greater stimulation and sensationalism, but as Eysenck and Nias (1978) have pointed out – little has been done to study the personality factor with regard to effects upon children or adults.

3 Context

Thirdly, there is the context in which the child sees the video. This may be done secretly – alone, or in groups of peers or in the company of a parent, or friend of the family or relative, commonly a male adult. Many parents hold the view that the frightening effects of some scenes in films or television can be effectively cancelled or at any rate eased, by explanation and reassurances. In particular many adults will comment about the scene not containing real characters.

Little research has been done however regarding the frightening effects of films or television on children. In a study by Cantor and Wilson (1984) comparisons were made in two age groups of three- to five-year-old and nine- to eleven-year-old children. A hundred and one children with their parents' permission, were shown chosen scenes from *The Wizard of Oz* and *The Incredible Hulk*. There was little evidence that the younger children benefited in any way from previous instructions whereas the older group of children did have some modification of their emotional responses by explanations given before the viewings. Such preparatory statements to the children were standardised and carefully worded. Assessments were made on the basis of self reports of emotional response.

What happened in a study of effects on forty-nine healthy undergraduates proved rather surprising, and the findings may also apply to children (Cantor, Ziemke and Sparks, 1984). Instead of a forewarning of the events in the horror film lessening the degree of fright and upset experienced, quite the opposite was found. Anxiety was heightened by such 'preparation'. If this happens to healthy undergraduates, it seems unlikely that much credence can be given to the popular and lighthearted response that children can easily be reassured about such things.

The disturbing effects of violent videos, in particular, are likely to remain in children's minds in spite of either forewarnings or reassurances. In recent months many school children have seen these videotapes without any kind of parental supervision or preparation or reassuring. Indeed it must be very difficult to convince a child that what has been seen in a violent video, such as described in Appendix 3 is not real. To make statements beforehand about the content of a tape cannot diminish the unfavourable effect in the child's mind. Nor can it be assumed that 'explanations' by the parents will smooth over the general effects of disturbance. The programme description on the cover of the videotape also cannot claim to have any minimising effect on viewers' mental or physiological reaction.

One argument may be to seek better techniques for immunising children against the disturbing and frightening effects of extremely violent videos. A simpler and surer method could be to stop the production of such material so that children and adolescents grow up without experiencing them.

Video Violence and the Lowering of Impulse Control

Some of the case reports we received gave account of a releasing effect on young persons or children who were under tension. Usually wayward, aggressive or delinquent behaviour had already taken place over a varying period of time before the impact of the video. There are instances where a situational crisis was followed by the viewing of horror videos. Then after a brief period, and sometimes within the same day, the individual would be triggered off into a series of behaviours culminating in an act of violence towards another person. The part played by the film or video appears contributory if not critical.

In the opinions of the interviewers the act of violence so resembled the scenes in the video described by the patient that a close association seemed obvious. In these cases there were other complex factors in the background, but expert opinion expressed to us emphasised that the existence of these factors need not and could not detract from the clear causal link between behaviour as viewed and behaviour as carried out.

Sexual, sadistic and violent motives and behaviour would in some cases all be mixed during a short period of time. Impulse control seems to have been lowered drastically by the video viewing, and assaults which were made, including stabbings, were seen to happen within a brief period of time after the viewing. The behaviour was sudden, often of short duration and consequent upon the film or video seen. It seems obvious from these cases that a combination of current tension and violent video viewing can combine and lead to impulsive acts of violence very similar to those in the video. Such attacks with stabbing were directed to adults and also in one case to a child and an adult. The closeness of the assault to the viewing of a particular video, strongly indicates an impulse release phenomenon, with suggestive impact upon the viewer. Such persons have limited or low impulse control, and while normally in command of their aggressive tendencies, these young persons can be precipitated into actions by viewing violence on their television screen while under stress. Based on the small number of cases described, it would seem likely that the future effects of such material would be to increase crimes of violence since individuals with poor impulse control, even while still in adolescence or childhood, have already been 'influenced to copy the film'.

Parallel to the specific acts of violence, there were cases where other behaviours of a destructive or aggressive nature took place in the same child/adolescent. There were instances of property destruction or fire raising, again apparently as impulsive acts. Such activities were not in the video programme, but were apparently associated because the disturbed behaviours followed one after the other until a specific act was carried out, for example, attack with a sharp instrument upon another child, a teacher or other adult, and the final behaviour reflected what had been seen in the film or video.

Drugs, Violence and Videos

Some writers reported the co-existence of these factors in a few cases, where crimes were committed in gangs, but it is too early to quantify the extent to which youths who gather together to watch pornographic or violent videos are at the same time participating in such activities as glue-sniffing or marijuana or heroin taking. With the advent of the violent video, it would seem prudent to ask young persons about their viewing habits when investigating an account of antisocial behaviour or drug taking. In this way we shall be able to obtain a fuller picture of the part played by the psychological effects of such films. There is so far in our reports no evidence that drug taking is followed by orgies of violent video viewing or the reverse. There has however been one case reported in the press where a pre-adolescent girl was given tranquillising pills 'in order to enable her to watch horror movies'. These were having an upsetting effect on the girl, and the mother gave her some of her own sedative prescription in order to counteract the emotional upheaval caused.

In some ways such action seems quite farcical, but some parents may be persuaded to give drugs since some children plead to be allowed to watch horror programmes while at the same time wishing to reduce their fright response. With so many homes now possessing tranquillisers there is a risk of other adults allowing the child to continue watching the scary film or video, while at the same time giving them their own tranquilliser medicine. The possibility of child-tranquillising because of reactions to video horror needs further investigating.

Present Cases and Future Trends

We have only been able to base information on a relatively small number of cases reported to us. These were the children and adolescents who were presented to clinics. For every case seen there are likely to be several others in the community. Many have features of anxiety; others have shown specific acts of violence precipitated by or copied from 'video nasties'. With the present rapid trend towards a widespread use of video recorders in the home it is possible that, as with television, most homes will in future have access to their own or hired video machine. How this machine is used, and what is shown on it will depend on a number of factors. One of the vital issues is the censorship and legality of films and tapes. This in turn will depend on what is considered to be harmful or undesirable for children and young persons, in any particular case.

In addition to the analysis on any one particular video, there are several other areas which need further investigation so far as the context in which video programmes are watched is concerned. One of these is the relation between overall provision of violence on the television screen, whether from television programmes, media films or videotape, and violence in society. Already much evidence has accrued in the USA regarding the trends of television violence and crimes of violence. This is referred to in Chapter 2.

A recent estimate in America indicates that twenty times as many films are now seen in the home as compared with the cinema. The number of films which exploited violence increased by fifty per cent in the one year 1980–81. In a previous decade, television violence trebled in the year 1956–57. This increase has continued and has maintained its high levels over the past two to three decades. Violence of all kinds as reported in the USA took an upward turn in the late '50s and has continued to rise since that time.

To what extent violent media and social violence is correlated will be a matter for debate and further investigation. These estimates from the National Coalition on Television Violence in America should be given careful consideration at a time when so little is still properly understood about the effect on the individual young person. The effects upon the older individual and especially on susceptible adults is another issue but not directly the concern of this volume. However, it must be realised that many of the adolescents affected by some video programmes will very soon be adults themselves.

Britain was recently claimed to be the top nation for density of home videos. If '18' rated films were to become more freely available, it is possible that forms of violence in the young would become more subtle, more sadistic, more associated with sexual behaviour, and potentially more disturbing to an increasing number of young persons. The trend at present is firmly in one direction. The violent video has portrayed all this in a new dimension. However, it can also be seen as the continuation of a trend which was first noted in the '50s. Now in the '80s the video explosion has arrived. The international extent of this has been featured in an article by *Newsweek* (No. 32, 6 August 1984).

Conclusion

The availability of home videos could become virtually universal in Britain, as the television has done over the past thirty years. It is no small or limited affair. Many homes now have more than one television set and the possibility of viewing of videos by children in their own rooms is becoming as commonplace as children viewing television today. The extent of this exposure to learning and to the moral teaching of the screen is great, and increasing year by year. **The video containing combinations of violence and sex is a potential mental and moral health hazard of a kind we have not experienced before.** Since the video is such a new phenomenon, reported cases of emotional disturbance and/or reactive behaviour are relatively few. Some idea of the nature of reported cases, but not their incidence has been presented in this chapter. We have attempted to abstract the main features that have emerged from brief studies sent to us by Child and Adolescent Psychiatrists.

We are grateful to those who have taken the trouble to send us case details as well as their opinions. At the same time we have been constrained to give a strict regard to case confidentiality and have therefore sought to avoid actual case descriptions in any detail. Our findings based on the cases given to us merely hint at what effects might be happening in children and adolescents, particularly those of a vulnerable disposition.

Acknowledgments

We are indebted to the many Child and Adolescent Psychiatrists who have made this chapter possible by their written observations, comments and opinions. We would also acknowledge with gratitude the co-operation of the Royal College of Psychiatrists and in particular the officers of the Child and Adolescent Section, who enabled us to circulate the membership of the Section with questionnaires which provided the case studies and data upon which this chapter is based.

References

BOZZUTO, J. C. (1975) 'Cinematic Neurosis following "The Exorcist"', *Journal of Nervous and Mental Diseases*.

CANTOR, J. 'Developmental Studies of Children's Fright from Mass Media', Presented Paper at The Convention of the International Communication Association, May 1982.

CANTOR, J. and REILLY, S. (1982) 'Adolescents' Fright Reactions to television and Films', *Journal of Communication*, 32:1, pp. 87–99.

CANTOR, J., ZIEMKE, D. and SPARKS, C. G. (1984) 'Effects of Forewarning on Emotional Responses to a Horror Film', *Journal of Broadcasting*, 28:1.

CARRUTHERS, M. and TAGGART, P. (1973) 'Vagotinicty of Violence: Biochemical and Cardiac Responses to Violent Films and Television Programmes', *British Medical Journal*, 3, 384.9.

EISENBERG, A. L. (1936) *Children and Radio Programmes*. Columbia University Press.

EYSENCK, H. J. and NIAS, D. K. (1978) *Sex, Violence and the Media*. Hounslow: Temple Smith.

HALLORAN, J. D. (1967) *Attitude Formation and Change*. Leicester University Press.

HAMBURG, D. A. (1971) Sir Geoffrey Vickers Lecture, London Mental Health Research Fund, quoted by Harrington (1972).

HIMMELWEIT, H. T., OPPENHEIM, A. N. and VINCE, P. (1958) *Television and the Child*. Oxford University Press.

MATHAI, J. (1983) 'An Acute Anxiety State in an Adolescent Precipitated by Viewing a Horror Movie', *Journal of Adolescence*, 6, pp. 197–200.

PRESTON, M. T. (1941) 'Children's Reactions to Movie Horrors and Radio Crime', *Journal of Paediatrics*, 19, pp. 147–68.

SINGER, J. L. (1975) *Daydreaming and Fantasy*. London: Allen and Unwin.

SINGER, J. L. (1973) *The Child's World of Make-believe: Experimental studies of imaginative play*. New York: Academic Press.

WERTHAM, F. (1953) *Seduction of the Innocent*. New York: Rhinehart.

8 Paediatricians' Survey

Peter Gray and Alison Hill

Introduction

The films which have been called 'video nasties' depict scenes of such horrific violence that they would not be granted a certificate to be screened at a cinema or on television. Yet these films, which were introduced into the United Kingdom as recently as 1982, rapidly became widely available through video shops, market stalls and many small vending agencies such as petrol stations and ice cream vans. The situation will be changed once the Video Recordings Act 1984 becomes operative. Unfortunately, but perhaps not surprisingly, many young children and teenagers have already seen these films. The research reported in *Video Violence and Children Part II* (1984) showed that a surprisingly high percentage of children between the ages of 7 and 16 have seen these and the '18' rated films which they would not be allowed legally to see at a cinema.

The reaction of people from many professions who work with children is that watching 'video nasty' films could be a potential cause of harm to a person of any age, but especially to a young child. It is important, therefore, to determine whether these videos have any effects and if so what the type and extent is. The effects, if any, could be immediate and/or longlasting. The immediate effects, if any, could well be disturbances of behaviour and personality easily recognisable to the parents, such as night terrors or expressed anxieties. The long term effects could be difficult both to ascertain and to disentangle from the many cultural, social, religious and family factors which interweave with the personality of a child during his maturation to adulthood.

One of the arguments which is given to allay fears about the potentially adverse effects of 'video nasties' is that children of all ages have been subjected to violence in the form of nursery rhymes and stories. Most nursery rhymes and fairy tales have a violent streak. The one great difference between violent stories of former years and those of this present era of films is that the former group are easily perceived by the child as within the realm of fantasy. Even so, some children may have acute reactions to fairy tales, such as night terrors, but these are unlikely to persist.

The nature of the violence portrayed in 'video nasties' is very distant from that in the fairy tales and nursery rhymes, or the violence in cartoons, or even the 'Hammer House of Horror' films shown on television. The 'video nasties' present violence of the crudest variety, often beyond the imagination of the average adult, which is portrayed in such a way that it appears to the child or adult to be completely real. These films show violence in explicit detail in real life situations with ordinary people. The characters portrayed are in many ways so 'normal' that many children come to identify themselves with the characters and **it is often the aggressor with whom they identify.**

Descriptions of the contents of some of the films are given in Appendix 3 of this book. The only side effects which could be ascertained adequately at the moment would be the acute problems because the films have been so recently available. It is likely that some disturbed children would be brought to the health visitor, the general practitioner, and possibly the paediatrician. It was decided to gather data from paediatricians on these films.

It was recognised that the information gained through such a survey would be based upon the opinions and experience of paediatricians, many of whom had not seen the videos nor had been previously aware of the possibility that children may have seen the films. It was thought likely that while a number of paediatricians would have been aware that children were seeing horrific films, they might not so far have seen children who had experienced any adverse effects from so doing. The object of the survey was to gather empirical evidence from those paediatricians who had seen children who had experienced various forms of effects, either good or bad, following viewing horrific violent video films. This survey is designed, therefore, to ascertain the opinions and experience of the doctors who work with school-age children concerning their observations of the effects on children of viewing violent videos. It is acknowledged that this survey lacks the precision of a full scale epidemiological community survey, nor does it have the scientific value of a randomised controlled trial (RCT). We nevertheless maintain that the former type of investigation is not warranted until there is some evidence of a cause and effect relationship being present, and this is precisely what the results of this survey provide. We also maintain that the idea of a RCT is so completely unethical as to be impracticable in the United Kingdom, as this would necessitate the deliberate exposure of children to scenes of violence in order to measure their reactions.

Methodology

Self-completion questionnaires were sent by post to members of the British Paediatric Association and the Community Paediatric Group in England and Wales. Efforts were made to restrict the circulation to those paediatricians engaged in clinical practice with children or adolescents so that they were able to base their opinions on their clinical experience. One thousand and ninety-two questionnaires were circulated and 413 questionnaires were returned completed, while 59 paediatricians returned uncompleted questionnaires for various reasons, mainly the fact that they did not see older children professionally who might be affected by violent videos, eg they were full-time neonatologists. Although only 37.8% of the total number of respondents circulated actually completed a questionnaire it was felt that this response was adequate. This compares favourably with another survey performed by the BPA which had a 32% completion race. F. N. Kerlinger (1973) in his book *Foundations of Behaviour of Research* states that 'returns of less than 40% or 50% are common. Higher percentages are rare. At best, the researcher must content himself with returns as low as 50% or 60%.' The professional status of the total number of respondents (413) is as follows:

222 Consultant Paediatricians
 56 Consultant Specialist Paediatricians
 38 Senior Registrars/Lecturers
 61 Senior Clinical Medical Officers
 14 Clinical Medical Officers
  4 Child Psychiatrists
  3 General Practitioners
 15 Others

The questionnaire was sent with a covering letter from Professor Peter Gray (Professor of Child Health, University of Wales College of Medicine) and the Lord Swinfen (Chairman of the Parliamentary Group Video Enquiry Working Party). The questionnaire (shown on page 137) was designed to discover the paediatricians' experience of children and filmed violence and their awareness, prior to the survey, of the role of violent videos in children's lives. It enquired whether their patients had viewed violent videos and whether they had ever thought that there was an association between their patients' symptoms and violent videos. Finally, it asked for their professional opinions on the effects on children of watching violent videos.

Definition

Throughout the questionnaire the term 'violent videos' was used. The definition of this term was given at the beginning of the questionnaire and is as follows:

The term 'violent videos' in the Parliamentary Group Video Enquiry refers to those video feature films which contain scenes of such violence and sadism involving either human beings or animals that they would not be granted a certificate for general release for public exhibition in Britain. It is **not** used to refer to pornography, either 'soft porn' or 'hard porn', unless violence and sadism are also involved.

Results

Four hundred and thirteen doctors completed the questionnaire. Two hundred and thirty paediatricians (55.7%) stated that they had been aware of the fact that violent videos were a factor in children's and adolescents' lives prior to this survey. Out of the paediatricians who had been aware of this new factor in children's lives, 89 paediatricians (38.7%) had been aware of it for over one year, while 85 paediatricians (37.0%) had been aware for more than six months but less than one year, 39 paediatricians (17.0%) had been aware for more than three months but less than six months and 17 paediatricians (7.4%) had been aware for less than three months.

No doctor thought that the viewing of 'video nasties' was either *often* or *always helpful*, when asked what they thought the effects upon children of seeing 'video nasties' were likely to be. Seventeen paediatricians (4.1%) thought that 'video nasties' were likely to be *sometimes helpful*, whereas the vast majority, 280 paediatricians, (67.8%) felt that 'video nasties' were likely to be *never* helpful. One hundred and sixteen paediatricians (28.1%) did not comment.

Fig. 8.1 *Percentage of respondents who thought that 'video nasties' were always, often, sometimes or never helpful*

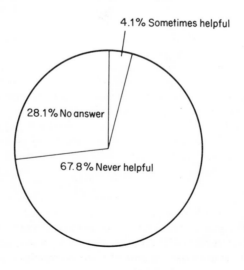

On the same question of what the effects upon children of seeing 'video nasties' are likely to be, three paediatricians (0.7%) thought that these films were likely to be *never harmful*. However the vast majority of paediatricians felt that 'video nasties' were a potential form of harm, with 147 paediatricians (35.6%) thinking they were *sometimes harmful*; 152 paediatricians (36.8%) thinking that they were *often harmful* and 72 paediatricians (17.4%) thinking that they were *always harmful*. Thirty-nine paediatricians (9.5%) gave no comment.

Fig. 8.2   *Percentage of respondents who thought that 'video nasties' were always, often, sometimes, or never harmful*

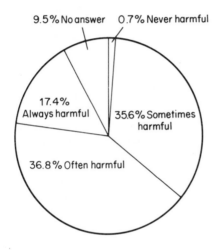

The enquiry sought to find out the doctors' practice with history taking, and 285 paediatricians (69.0%) said that they had never asked whether any of their disturbed patients had ever viewed, or viewed regularly, violent videos. One hundred and fourteen paediatricians (27.6%) said that they occasionally enquired, and only 14 paediatricians (3.4%) said that they usually enquired.

The respondents were asked whether in the last year they had received any accounts from a parent/guardian about a violent video being influential on his/her child's emotional state or behaviour. Three hundred and fifty-five paediatricians (86.0%) said that they had never received any accounts of this nature, while 55 paediatricians (13.3%) said that they had received accounts of this nature from parents of at least one but less than five different patients, and three paediatricians (0.7%) said that they had received accounts from parents of between five and ten patients. No paediatrician had received accounts about more than ten patients.

Out of the 58 paediatricians who had received accounts from a parent/ guardian about a violent video being influential on his/her child's emotional state or behaviour, 31 paediatricians (53.4%) said that the children's behaviour had worsened following seeing a violent video; ten paediatricians (17.2%) said that the behaviour had remained the same, while no paediatrician felt that a child's behaviour had improved following seeing a violent video.

The respondents were also asked whether they had ever thought there was any association between any of their particular patients' descriptions of their symptoms or the symptoms they exhibited, and their viewing violent videos. 351 paediatricians (85.0%) said that they had never thought there was any association, while 61 paediatricians (14.8%) had thought there was an association in less than five different patients and one paediatrician (0.2%) had thought there was an association in between five and ten patients. No paediatrician had thought there was an association in more than ten patients.

Out of the 62 paediatricians who had found associations between their patients' symptoms and their viewing violent videos, 18 paediatricians (29.0%) felt that the symptoms were definitely precipitated by violent videos and 36 paediatricians (58.1%) felt that the symptoms were possibly precipitated by violent videos. Twenty-three paediatricians (37.1%) thought that existing symptoms had been worsened by viewing violent videos, while 10 paediatricians (16.1%) thought that the existing symptoms had been unchanged by watching violent videos. No paediatrician felt that the existing symptoms had been ameliorated by watching violent videos and 29 paediatricians did not comment.

The question of whether paediatricians had considered violent videos to be a factor in children's lives prior to this survey is of major importance in influencing their answers to other questions. For example, only 31.0% of all respondents in the survey said that they usually or occasionally enquired whether their patients ever viewed violent videos. However, 48.6% of those respondents who were aware prior to the survey, usually or occasionally enquired.

Similarly those who enquired about their patients' viewing patterns were more likely than those who did not to receive an account about a violent video being influential in a patient's life or to think there was an association between the patient's symptoms and viewing violent videos. While only 14.0% and 15.0% of all respondents in the survey had received an account and found an association respectively, when only those respondents who usually or occasionally enquired about their patients' viewing patterns are taken into account these percentages increase to 38.7% for receiving an account and 41.1% for finding an association between a patient's symptoms and his viewing violent videos.

It seems, therefore, that the more a doctor enquires about the viewing of violent videos, the more likely he is to have experience of patients being affected by viewing them.

The following figures relate to only those respondents who enquired whether their patients viewed violent videos and/or had experience of violent videos affecting their patients' lives. In the survey there were 67 paediatricians who had enquired but had 'no experience', 61 paediatricians who had enquired *and* had 'experience', and 11 paediatricians who had never enquired but nevertheless had 'experience'. Therefore, there were 139 paediatricians who had enquired and/or had 'experience'. These 139 respondents form a sub-sample which is 34% of the total sample. The professional composition of this sub-sample is basically similar to that of the total sample (see page 124) with the exception of there being relatively fewer consultants and more senior clinical medical officers in the sub-sample.

Out of the 139 paediatricians who had enquired and/or had 'experience', 116 paediatricians (83.5%) had considered violent videos to be a factor in children's and adolescents' lives prior to this survey. Forty-six paediatricians (39.7%) had considered this more than one year ago, while 45 paediatricians (38.8%) had considered this more than six months ago but less than one year ago, while the rest had considered it less than six months ago.

When asked what they thought the effects upon children of seeing 'video nasties' were likely to be, none of the paediatricians in this sub-sample felt that the effects were likely to be *always* or *often helpful*, but nine paediatricians (6.5%) felt that 'video nasties' were likely to be *sometimes helpful*. The vast majority of paediatricians in this sub-sample, however, felt the 'video nasties' were likely to be *never helpful* (98 paediatricians, 70.5%). Thirty-two paediatricians (23.0%) did not comment.

Twenty-five paediatricians (18.0%) felt that the effects upon children of seeing 'video nasties' were likely to be *always harmful*; 56 paediatricians (40.3%) felt that 'video nasties' were *often harmful* and 48 paediatricians (34.5%) felt that 'video nasties' were *sometimes harmful*. No paediatrician in the sub-sample felt that 'video nasties' were *never harmful* while ten paediatricians did not comment.

The paediatricians were asked what, in their opinion, based on their practice rather than on what the media had said, were the effects on children of viewing violent videos. The answers to this question are only being reported for those paediatricians who had enquired and/or had 'experience' since it was necessary for the paediatricians' answers to be based on their own experience. One paediatrician (0.7%) thought that viewing violent videos was *usually beneficial* or reassuring for children while no paediatrician felt that viewing violent videos was *occasionally beneficial* or reassuring. Over half the paediatricians who had enquired and/or had 'experience' felt that the effects on children of viewing violent videos were harmful or disturbing. Fifty paediatricians (36.0%) felt that viewing violent videos was *occasionally harmful* or disturbing while 24 paediatricians (17.3%) felt that viewing violent videos was *usually harmful* or disturbing. Five paediatricians (3.6%) felt that viewing violent videos was neither beneficial nor harmful while 59 paediatricians (42.4%) gave no comment.

Fig. 8.3 *Percentage of respondents who thought that viewing violent videos was harmful or beneficial*

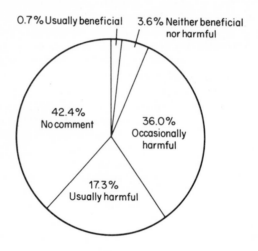

Only two paediatricians (1.4%) in this sub-sample of paediatricians who had enquired and/or had 'experience' had ever found a patient who had shown a reduction in violent behaviour following violent videos. Nineteen paediatricians (13.7%) had found a patient who had shown an increase in violent behaviour following viewing violent videos.

Discussion

The results of this survey are very interesting. Over 55% of the 413 respondents had been aware before the survey of the role that violent videos may play in children's and adolescents' lives and the vast majority (75%) of them had known about this for more than six months. In the sub-sample of those respondents who had enquired whether their patients viewed violent videos and/or had experience of violent videos affecting their patients' lives, over 83% had been aware that violent videos were a significant factor in children's lives prior to this survey.

Harmful effects

Over 67% of the respondents thought that the effects upon children of seeing 'video nasties' were likely to be *never helpful*, while only 4% of the respondents thought that 'video nasties' were likely to be *sometimes helpful*, and no-one thought that these films were likely to be *often* or *always helpful*. In the sub-sample over 70% of the respondents thought that 'video nasties' were likely to be *never helpful*, 6.5% of the respondents believed that 'video nasties' were *sometimes helpful* and no-one considered that these films were *always* or *often helpful*. Only nine respondents in the sub-sample thought that 'video nasties' were *sometimes helpful* and some of these qualified this statement by saying that they felt completely neutral (ie sometimes helpful; sometimes harmful).

Seventeen per cent of the total number of respondents thought that 'video nasties' were likely to be *always harmful*, while the majority thought they were likely to be *often* (36.8%) or *sometimes* (35.6%) *harmful*. Only three respondents thought that 'video nasties' were likely to be *never harmful*, and all three of these had never enquired whether any of their disturbed patients had ever viewed, or viewed regularly, violent videos. All three thought that 'video nasties' were likely to be *never helpful* as well as *never harmful*. In the sub-sample of respondents who had 'enquired' and/or had 'experience' 18% thought that 'video nasties' were likely to be *always harmful*. Forty per cent thought that 'video nasties' were likely to be *often harmful* and 34.5% thought that 'video nasties' were likely to be *sometimes harmful*. No respondent in this sub-sample thought that 'video nasties' were likely to be *never harmful*.

Even though over 55% of the total number of respondents in this survey had been aware for at least a month prior to this survey of violent videos being a factor in children's and adolescents' lives, only 31% of the respondents had enquired whether any of their disturbed patients had ever viewed, or viewed regularly, violent videos.

Parents' reports

Fourteen per cent of the total number of respondents had received accounts from a parent/guardian about a violent video being influential on his/her child's emotional state of behaviour. However, 39% of those respondents who enquired whether any of their disturbed patients had ever viewed, or viewed regularly violent videos had received accounts from a parent/guardian about a violent video being influential on his/her child's emotional state or behaviour. Similarly, 15% of the total number of respondents had thought that there was an association between one or more of their patients' description of their symptoms or the symptoms they exhibit and their viewing violent videos, while over 41% of those respondents who had enquired about their patients' viewing patterns had noted an association. It seems that those children's doctors who enquired about their patients' viewing patterns were much more likely to associate some of their patients' symptoms with their viewing violent videos.

Paediatricians' experience

The respondents in the sub-sample who had enquired and who had some experience of children's viewing habits were asked what were the effects on children of viewing violent videos. The answer to this question was based on the doctors' experience through their practice rather than on what the media had said. Forty-two per cent of these respondents gave no answer to this question, usually because they felt they did not have enough experience. The majority of the respondents felt that the effects on children of viewing violent videos were either *occasionally harmful or disturbing* (36.0%) or *usually harmful or disturbing* (17.3%). Five respondents (3.6%) felt that the effects on children were *neither beneficial nor harmful* and one respondent felt that the effects on children were *usually beneficial or reassuring*.

This paediatrician who felt that the effects on children of viewing violent videos were *usually beneficial or reassuring* occasionally enquired whether any of his patients had viewed, or viewed regularly, violent videos, but had never found any association between any of his patients' symptoms and their viewing violent videos. He commented that his view was that 'a lot of teenagers are able to get rid of a lot of aggression by watching these rather than by going out and being incredibly violent'. This sort of view is often called the cathartic effect of seeing aggression.

Those respondents who had the experience of violent videos being influential on children's lives were asked whether the children's behaviour following seeing a violent video *improved, remained the same* or *worsened*, and whether the symptoms were *precipitated* by violent videos or whether the existing symptoms were *altered* by violent videos. The most common symptoms that were cited as being *precipitated* by violent videos were sleep disturbances.

Sleeplessness, nightmares, bed-wetting and even night terrors were often noted. One doctor had reports from two parents of children experiencing fearfulness, regression to much younger behaviour and depression, and commented that these symptoms seem to have been precipitated by sadistic video films. Fearfulness and anxiety about being alone, especially in the dark, seem to be very common symptoms. One doctor cited the case of an 11-year-old boy who had twice been unexpectedly exposed to violent videos at a friend's house. Each time he had left the house and had run home absolutely terrified. The child developed late night waking: crying and running into his mother's room. This persisted for a short time after each exposure and then calmed down. The child also became very frightened to be alone in his own home or visit the lavatory without a friendly adult as he feared what might happen to him on the way. This symptom was still persisting one year after the exposure.

Personality and intelligence

The effects of violent videos upon children must vary greatly, dependent upon the individual personality differences of the children and their up-bringing. One doctor thought that 'the girls appear genuinely disturbed by the films and the boys not so'. However, there are many other factors involved in a child's personal make-up, besides sex, that influence the way he or she reacts to violence. Age, for example, is a very important factor. Older children may be able to cope more effectively than younger children with the violence that they see. One doctor concluded that 'for the majority of children there are inbuilt defence mechanisms which allow compensation for the input of horror and pornography. However, I think there are some susceptible children and adults who do not have this facility and who will be permanently damaged.'

Intelligence may be another important factor that may influence the way a child will react to violence. Less intelligent children may not have the same ability to subdue the tendency to copy seen behaviour. For example, a doctor had seen a 19-year-old boy who, directly after watching a video at a friend's house, went home and repeated the incident he had seen in the film by raping his 13-year-old step-sister. The boy admitted that he had been influenced by the video film he had just seen. However, this boy had a low IQ and came from a deprived family background and both of these factors may have had some influence on the child's behaviour.

The personality of a child also affects the way he or she reacts to violence. For example, there is a tendency for more emotionally-sensitive people (ie high Neuroticism (N) scores in the Eysenck Personality Questionnaire) to perceive violent scenes as more frightening or personally disturbing than less-sensitive individuals (Gunter and Furnham, 1983).

Family background

Family background seems to be a particularly important factor in that children are brought up with different values and different attitudes towards violence. Many children see so much real violence within their own homes that they become desensitised to it and grow up thinking that violence is part of life. In such cases the violence they see on television and video is part of life and may have little effect other than reinforcing their own already estab-lished values and opinions. Indeed one doctor felt that the vast majority of violent children she had seen in the last ten years had been 'taking their cue from their parents rather than the television'.

The family background and the attitude of the parents towards violence influences the make-up of the child and confounds any cause and effect explanations of a violent outburst/disturbance. This was the case with a teenage girl who had anxiety problems after watching a film about a mother's throat being cut. The girl had been involved in her parents' marital break-up and had watched the film with her antagonistic father. The father was extremely violent and would often 'take it out' on his daughter. The doctor who dealt with the case says that 'the social situation was particularly bad but the film she watched "damaged" her further'.

One doctor concluded by saying, 'I am convinced in my mind that watching ordinary violent films on television increases the tendency to violence, depending on the home background and the stability and security in the home together with the parents' attitudes.' It seems that the family background and social situation are two major factors that could influence the way that children react to violence. In the experience of another doctor, 'it is the chaotic families about which we already have grave concerns who are heavy users of videos of all types; such families are unlikely to protect their young children from viewing unsuitable material'. It may well be that families who enjoy watching violent videos are likely to be violent themselves.

Propensity to violence

This raises the question of whether there are some people who have a greater appetite for violence than others. Do some viewers actively seek and enjoy watching violence, and if so, do they already have an aggressive nature? To what extent is the correlation between viewing violence and aggressive or delinquent behaviour due to the viewers being predisposed to violence and to what extent is the relationship due to the exposure to violence leading to an increased propensity towards violence in the viewer? See Eron, 1963; Dominick and Greenberg, 1972; McIntyre and Teevan, 1972; McLeod *et al.*, 1972.

There have been a number of research studies on the subject of violence and its influence on behaviour. From these there have emerged three contrasting views which may be summarised as follows:

1 There have been many research observations which have found that watching violence leads to aggressive behaviour.
2 Some researchers have not been able to demonstrate that watching violence has any effect on the viewer.
3 Some researchers have argued that watching violence actually decreases the viewer's propensity towards violence.

The evidence from this survey of paediatricians in England and Wales tends to support the first of these views in that it demonstrates that the viewing of scenes of violence has a harmful effect on many children. One doctor summed up his view by saying, 'Our lives and attitudes are influenced by our experiences and it seems obvious to me that bad experiences will not be beneficial. The viewing of violence, etc. on television, particularly as it is shown as entertainment and not as an example of something to be avoided will, inevitably, have a bad effect on children.' Another concluded that 'Basic common sense would make one guess that the more violence is seen, the more it may be adopted as part of behaviour.'

Imitative behaviour

Watching violence on video can have a bad effect on children not only by frightening them but also by encouraging them to be violent and teaching them aggressive ways. Everyone is influenced by what they see and experience. Children in particular may imitate the behaviour they see on television and video. One consultant paediatrician illustrated this by recording children from one family who were found by the parents to be playing with drills. The children regularly played with the drills (without switching on the power) and pretended to kill each other. The children had seen similar behaviour on a video film entitled *Driller Killer*. This paediatrician also cited a number of other cases in which children had been affected by watching violent videos and said that he had seen 'no direct clinical *illness* from "video nasty" exposure, but plenty of associated behaviour'.

A senior lecturer in community paediatrics said, 'We are beginning to see quite young children and some older, mentally handicapped children trying to act out the scenes they have seen portrayed.' However, it is not just the very young children who might imitate the type of behaviour they see on video films. A consultant paediatrician cited the case of one of his patients, aged 15, who had just been convicted of murder, having repeatedly stabbed an eight-year-old boy. The boy was described as a loner with problems of reasoning who 'fantasised about violence'. He both read a lot of horror books, and regularly and frequently watched violent horrific video films. Concern was expressed that his interest in horror seemed to go beyond the typical fascination with this sort of material at his age, but before the assessment had been completed, he was arrested for the murder of the eight-year-old boy, for which he was subsequently convicted.

Desensitisation

One of the effects of repeated exposure to violent videos may be to desensitise children to violence. Children who were once shocked at the violence that they see on video films may now feel that such violence is a part of everyday life. One specialist in Community Medicine, describing the effects on children and young people who watch violent videos, said 'certainly their sensitivity to violence must be very much blunted and their respect for human beings and animals eroded', while another paediatrician felt that the 'debasing of human sensitivity and empathy is inevitable with a heavy exposure'.

Fantasy and reality

Continually viewing violent scenes on television or video can also distort children's views about the 'real world'. Many children who do not possess the adult degree of sophistication, may not realise that the fantasy they see in the video films bears only a slight resemblance to the real world. One clinical medical officer cited the case of a four-year-old child whose conversations included references to violent videos and he noted that these videos **'appear to be indistinguishable from reality to the child'**. A community paediatrician has also noted that **some primary school children have trouble in distinguishing between fantasy and reality**, and the real hurt from the pretend.

One paediatrician, however, claims that violent videos can be harmful but most children can differentiate between reality and fantasy. He says all children have an active fantasy world. Whilst this is certainly true for many children, there may be some who are not capable of making such a distinction. One consultant paediatrician stated that **'acceptance of violence alters the perception of children as to the realities of physical injuries**. Children may be seriously frightened as the reality and the video become confused.'

Long-term Effects

It seems from the comments and conclusions obtained through this survey that children's doctors are very concerned about the effects that watching violent videos could have on some children. One paediatrician had seen a selection of scenes from about eight 'video nasties'. She said she was deeply shocked and sickened by what she had seen, and for about two weeks after this found that her sleep was being disturbed by nightmare recollections. She says that these video films 'must be as harmful to immature adults as to children' and that 'right minded people can have no concept of the content of these films'. Another consultant said that **'scenes of violence cannot be good for anyone and must be harmful to emotionally immature human beings'** while another paediatrician says, 'I am absolutely sure that to some children, such exposure is extremely traumatic and very long lasting . . . 20 years in practice leaves me in no doubt whatsoever that **some children exposed to "video nasties" will be very seriously and perhaps permanently damaged'**.

Summary

1 56% of the paediatricians who responded to this survey had been aware prior to the survey that violent videos are a significant factor in children's and adolescents' lives.

2 31% of respondents usually or occasionally enquired whether their patients had ever viewed, or regularly viewed violent videos. However, almost 50% of respondents who had been aware of violent videos being a factor in children's lives prior to the survey, enquired about their patients' viewing patterns.

3 14% of respondents had received accounts about a patient whose emotional state or behaviour had been influenced by watching a violent video. However, almost 40% of those respondents who enquired about their patients' viewing patterns had received similar accounts.

4 15% of respondents had thought that there was an association between the symptoms of at least one of their patients and their viewing violent videos. However, 41% of those respondents who enquired about their patients' viewing patterns had found similar associations between their patients' symptoms and violent videos.

5 Almost 70% of the paediatricians in the survey held the opinion that the viewing of 'video nasties' was likely to be never helpful, while only 4% thought that it could be sometimes helpful and no respondent thought that 'video nasties' could be often or always helpful.

6 Less than 1% of respondents thought that 'video nasties' were likely to be never harmful, while 90% of respondents thought that 'video nasties' were likely to be at least sometimes harmful, with 17% believing that they were always harmful.

7 Out of those respondents who had enquired about their patients' viewing patterns and had experience of violent videos being influential on, or associated with a patient's symptoms, over 53% felt that from their experience the viewing of violent videos is either occasionally or usually harmful, while only 46% were neutral and only one respondent felt that viewing violent videos is either occasionally or usually beneficial or reassuring.

Acknowledgments

We would like to thank all the members of the British Paediatric Association who participated in this survey by providing information about their professional experience with children.

References

DOMINICK, J. and GREENBERG, B. S. (1972) 'Attitudes towards violence: Interaction of television, social class, and family attitudes', in CORNSTOCK, G. and RUBINSTEIN, E. A. (eds) *Television and Social Behaviour: Vol. 3, Television and Adolescent Aggressiveness.* Washington DC: US Government Printing Office.

ERON, L. D. (1963) 'Relationship of TV viewing habits and aggressive behaviour in children', *Journal of Abnormal and Social Psychology*, 67, pp. 193–8.

GUNTER, B. and FARNHAM, A. 'Personality and the perception of TV violence', *Personality, and Individual Differences. Vol. 4*, No. 3, pp. 315–321.

LIEBERT and POULOS (1976) 'Television as a Moral Teacher', in LICHONA, T. (ed) *Moral Development and Behaviour: theory, research and social issues.* New York: Holt, Rinehart and Winston.

MCINTYRE, J. and TEEVAN, J. (1972) 'Television violence and deviant behaviour', in CORNSTOCK, G. A. and RUBINSTEIN, E. A. op. cit.

MCLEOD, J., ATKIN, C. and CHAFFEE, S. (1972) 'Adolescents, parents and television use', in CORNSTOCK, G. A. and RUBINSTEIN, E. A. op. cit.

Department of Child Health, Welsh National School of Medicine Survey of Children's Viewing Patterns in Association with the Parliamentary Group Video Enquiry

The term 'violent videos' in the Parliamentary Group Video Enquiry refers to those video feature films which contain scenes of such violence and sadism involving either human beings or animals that they would not be granted a certificate for general release for public exhibition in Britain. It is **not** used to refer to pornography either 'soft porn' or 'hard porn' unless violence and sadism are also involved.
(Please CIRCLE the appropriate response)

1 Do you enquire whether any of your disturbed patients have ever viewed, or view regularly, violent videos?
   Never 1
   Occasionally 2
   Usually 3

2a In the last year have you received any accounts from a parent/guardian about a violent video being influential on his/her child's emotional state or behaviour?
   Never 1
   Less than 5 different patients 2
   5–10 patients 3
   More than 10 patients 4

2b Have you encountered children whose behaviour following seeing a violent video has:
   Improved 1
   Remained the same 2
   Worsened 3

If you have observed change, could you give brief details below.

....

....

....

3 Have you thought there was ANY association between any of your particular
   patients' descriptions of their symptoms or the symptoms they exhibit and their
   viewing violent videos?

   Never 1
   Less than 5 different patients 2
   5–10 patients 3
   More than 10 patients 4

   If you have thought there was an association, could you give brief details below:-

   ....

   ....

   ....

   If so,

   (a) did you think symptoms were precipitated by violent videos?
        Yes 1
        Possibly 2
        No 3
        Not applicable 4

   (b) did you think existing symptoms were altered by violent videos?
        Symptoms ameliorated 1
        Symptoms unchanged 2
        Symptoms worsened 3
        Not applicable 4

4 In your opinion, based on your practice rather than what the media have said, has
   the effect on children of viewing violent videos been?

   Usually beneficial or reassuring 1
   Occasionally beneficial or reassuring 2
   Neither beneficial nor harmful 3
   Occasionally harmful or disturbing 4
   Usually harmful or disturbing 5
   Other (please specify) 6

5a Have you ever found a patient who has shown a reduction in violent behaviour
   following viewing violent videos?

   Yes 1
   No 2

   If yes
   Frequently 1
   Occasionally 2
   Not applicable 3

5b Have you ever found a patient who has shown an increase in violent behaviour following viewing violent videos?

Yes 1
No 2

If yes

Frequently 1
Occasionally 2
Not applicable 3

6a Due to the fact that the violent video is a recent phenomenon in Britain many professional people have not been aware of it being a factor in children's and adolescents' lives. Had you considered it prior to this survey?

Yes 1
No 2

6b If yes, could you give some indication of how long ago you first became aware of this?

More than a week ago 1
More than a month ago 2
More than 3 months ago 3
More than 6 months ago 4
More than a year ago 5

7 Approximately how many new inpatients and outpatients per week do you see personally?

0–6 years ....
7–12 years ....
13–16 years ....

8 Do you think that the effects upon children of seeing video nasties are likely to be:

Always helpful 1
Often helpful 2
Sometimes helpful 3
Never helpful 4
Never harmful 1
Sometimes harmful 2
Often harmful 3
Always harmful 4

9 My NHS appointment is:

Consultant (General Paediatrics) 1
Consultant (Specialist Paediatrics) 2
Senior Registrar 3
Senior Clinical Medical Officer 4
Surgeon 5
Other (please specify) 6

....
....
....

9 Educationalists' Report

Pat Wynnejones

Introduction

The purpose of this Educationalists' Report is not to provide further statistical evidence on schoolchildren's viewing patterns, but rather to provide additional data and a commentary upon the evidence already produced through the National Viewers' Survey. This is not a statistical report, and therefore no attempt has been made to quantify the teachers' responses to measure how representative they are.

The head teachers and teachers in all the schools that took part in the National Viewers' Survey were asked to supply evidence through self-completed questionnaires and accompanying reports on class discussions, children's art, essays, classroom behaviour and patterns of play that revealed any evidence of the effects of watching violent video films. Teachers in other schools throughout England and Wales were invited through Teachers' Associations to participate by submitting evidence for this Report. The enquiry was carried out between November 1983 and November 1984.

The evidence presented in this Report will be seen to be one-sided. That is not because the evidence has been manipulated, but simply because no teacher has submitted any evidence to suggest that the viewing of violent video films is beneficial to children. It is, of course, possible to argue that teachers who had such evidence withheld it, and only those teachers with evidence of the harmful effects of violent video films took the trouble to submit it. In our opinion such a view is untenable in the face of the overwhelming evidence that was submitted to us. The data presented in this chapter is based upon the professional records and opinions of experienced teachers covering the whole age range of schoolchildren throughout the different regions of Britain.

This Report is intended to serve as an adjunct to the statistical analysis of data on children's viewing patterns summarised in Chapter 4 of this book. When the results of that survey were first published in March 1984 there were some, both within and outside the teaching profession, who expressed surprise that such a high proportion of schoolchildren had seen one or more

of the video films that were the subject of proceedings under the Obscene
Publications Act 1959. The evidence in this Report gives overwhelming
support to the fact that large numbers of children have been seeing these
violent films. It also presents evidence of the effects upon the lives and
behaviour of large numbers of children. Indeed, it is possible that during the
few years that uncensored video films have been freely available throughout
Britain, a whole generation of schoolchildren have experienced, either at first
hand, or through interaction with other children, a social phenomenon that
has radically affected their social and moral values.

Independent Surveys

Following the publication of the results of the Parliamentary Group's
Report, many schools, and in some cases all the schools in a town, carried out
their own independent surveys and enquiries to test the situation among
their children. Typical of the reports we received of these enquiries is the
following from the deputy headmaster of a large London comprehensive
school.

> I can well appreciate how many parents and teachers who studied the
> startling figures in *Video Violence and Children* that were published in
> March 1984 found them too bad to be true! Could it really be that 45% of
> the nation's children have seen violent rape and brutal murder portrayed
> on the screen in their homes? Furthermore, it is perhaps understandablde
> that some find it difficult to believe that a fleeting glance of such sex and
> violence on a video should have a lastingly adverse effect on boys and girls
> in an enlightened age. I wondered myself whether the 'normal' pupils
> facing me each day across the classroom in my respected West London
> Comprehensive School could have had such searing experiences? Surely
> not! I decided to do my own enquiry and was in for a nasty shock. The
> results of a survey on 73 15-year-old pupils, chosen at random, revealed
> that 63 of them (84%) had seen at least one of the 51 banned films on the
> DPP's list. Four of the pupils had seen over 20 of these films.

The reaction of surprise concerning children's viewing habits was fairly
typical among teachers before the publication of the first of the Parliamentary Group's Reports and the widespread discussion of the subject in the
media. We received many reports from teachers indicating that they had
been unaware that the children in their classes were watching violent videos.
We published some of these comments in the earlier Reports. Typical was
the teacher of a South London Comprehensive school with a class of fourth
year mixed boys and girls. He wrote:

> This is quite a 'nice' class by this school's standards. In discussion
> afterwards I was quite surprised. They nearly all prefer the horror films.

They like the blood and they didn't think that 'video nasties' should be banned. For most there was no parental control over television or video viewing. Most parents would allow younger children to watch violent videos.

Children's Viewing Patterns

During the course of the various stages of the Video Enquiry, a considerable body of empirical evidence has been gathered from the written comments of children on their completed questionnaires and from essays sent to us by teachers. This has proved to be valuable confirmation of the teachers' reports of class discussions and the verbal comments of the children.

The following is a 'selection' of quotes from teachers' reports.

I (and my colleagues) are becoming increasingly alarmed at the way young children are given access to 'X' rated video films. We have noticed that children who watch such films become very nervous, excessively bite fingernails, and become withdrawn. One *infant* child who is exposed to pornographic material has become very disruptive and violent.

I have a class of 7- and 8-year-olds and have become increasingly worried about the films they tell me they watch. Several children were discussing how frightened they had become by watching *An American Werewolf in London* at another child's birthday party. On another occasion a girl told me that she had screamed so much whilst watching *Friday 13th* that she had to be slapped.

Recently I was deeply disturbed to discover that a group of 9-year-old boys in my class were frequently allowed to watch videos hired by their parents. Most of these were normally classified as 'horror films' (*Halloween II, The Exorcist*, etc.). However, at least three had seen *The Texas Chain Saw Massacre* and one boy's father had hired the banned *Driller Killer*, about which horrific scenes were recounted in detail by the boy in question.

In our primary school it is the poorer families who seem to have videos, often with several children, extra busy mums, etc. These children often talk about seeing horror-type films. As a parent, I have personally experienced two unfortunate incidents where my 9-year-old son has visited a friend's house and has been shown video horror films, completely unsuitable for children (*Omen 2* and *An American Werewolf in London*). My son was terrified on both occasions, after only a few minutes' watching, and there were problems for several nights at bedtime, and afterwards for some time (he is an ordinary, tough boy who loves science fiction etc. at his level).

Several of my colleagues and I have found even primary-aged children rent 'X' type films to show on videos when their parents are out. In certain families the children watch these films with their parents. In one particular case they have 'porn on Fridays' because the father would rather his 12-year-old son watched such films with his parents, than secretly with friends. Many children (again including the under-11s) have bedroom television sets and watch video 'horrors' etc. on their own there.

During the last academic year I taught 10- and 11-year-olds and I was appalled by what they were allowed to see. This year I'm teaching 7- and 8-year-olds and as you can imagine, the problem is even more worrying. My main concern is not the children who view unsuitable material in secret, although this obviously happens. What is particularly worrying is the fact that parents allow, condone and encourage their children to view with them. The films are usually cinema certificated but are very often 'X' certificate, containing scenes of mindless violence, explicit sex and foul language. In my experience, the weekly or weekend film is chosen by the parents principally for them but they would never think to exclude the rest of the family or send the children to bed, especially as they often view at any time during the day. I have spoken to a number of parents about their attitude purely on a conversational level. The majority seem to take no notice of the cinema rating. One or two have said that they do not worry about explicit sexual content as their children (10- and 11-year-olds) 'know all about that'! Horror films are popular and children are allowed to view unattended, presumably because the adults concerned think that the children will be able to view on a superficial level which in my opinion they cannot. One mother was slightly concerned to find out that *An American Werewolf in London*, bought as a horror film, had its final scenes in a Piccadilly Circus 'porn' cinema, with the film as the background scene but she soon dismissed it because her child knew all about the facts of life!

There is considerable evidence for horror films being the most popular with children of all ages. Our analysis of the data indicates that approximately half of children of junior age regard horror films as their favourite while as many as three-quarters of children of secondary age prefer horror to any other kind of film.

It appears that even quite young children have a fascination for the kind of film sequences that scare them. Even if they watch with hands covering their face, squinting through the cracks in their fingers, or from behind an armchair, they still must watch. Typical is the comment of the little 9-year-old girl who said, 'I like scaring myself and I like looking at blood. When I watch horror videos I sit and peel my cuts.'

The most violent and horrific film sequences are the ones that make the most vivid impression upon the child's mind and are the most remembered. The following are all comments by children in class discussions on their most remembered films sequences. They come from a class of juniors aged 9 and 10 and are all taken from the class teacher's report.

A 10-year-old boy said the sequence he remembered most was 'the bit in *SS Experiment Camp* where a man had his eyes burnt out'. But he added, 'I am not allowed to watch *Texas Chain Saw Massacre* again.' He didn't say why. A girl said, 'In *Zombie Terror* something came out of a river and bit a lady's arm off.' Another child said, 'A man's insides were ripped out and turned around in the air.' A boy said, 'I like the blood bits. There was this man who pushed his hands in someone's stomach and when he pulled his arms out his hands weren't there.'

Other comments were, 'A machine chopped a man's hands off and they crawled along the floor.' 'There was this man running after a woman who opened a cupboard door and a body full of nails fell out.' 'There was a man who chopped a body into pieces.' 'The lady turned into a big spider and stabbed people and sucked their blood.' 'A man's head is chopped off and lands on a tree and the headless body walks off.'

All the above were quotes from one class, but they could be duplicated from many other class reports. The majority of children in the class discussions appeared to prefer video to television. The usual comments on this subject are that 'TV is boring, you don't get much choice on TV whereas you get a much greater range of films on video.' 'You can choose what you want and when you want to see it.' By far the most repeated answer on this subject was that videos can be stopped and replayed over favourite scenes. 'You can see the head chopped off over and over again.' 'You can use the fast forward to see what is going to happen and when the scary bits come.'

Sex Films

The age of the child is an important variable in the children's viewing patterns. For example, with secondary age children there is clear evidence of considerable interest in pornographic films. The list of favourite films whose titles were written out by hand by the children in one class of 13- and 14-year-olds of mixed sexes, were almost all either pornographic or horror video films. The most popular titles on the list were *Insatiable*, *Phantasm*, *Halloween*, *The Warriors*, *House Near the Cemetery*, *The Wanderers*, *Concrete Jungle*, *Lemon Popsicle*, *Hot Bubblegum*, *Going Steady*, *American Graffiti*, *Emmanuelle II*, *Boys From Company Three*, and *Confessions of a Window Cleaner*. One 15-year-old girl wrote on her questionnaire that her most remembered video was 'a sex film, probably illegal'.

It is probably only a small minority of younger children who watch pornographic films. From the teachers' reports we do have some evidence of parents either allowing children to watch this type of video or deliberately exposing them to them. But the children's own comments indicate that juniors much prefer horror films of the *Zombie Creeping Flesh* type or the cannibalistic type. Many of these films do, however, depict explicit sex or even rape scenes so that it cannot be assumed that children below teenage are not being exposed to pornographic or deviant sex films.

Restrictions on Viewing

One of the major findings of the National Viewers' Survey conducted for the Parliamentary Group was the evidence it provided on parental control of children's viewing habits. The survey revealed that most parents do exercise some control and place restrictions on their children's television viewing below the age of 12. For children above the age of 12 there appeared to be few restrictions. The same patterns emerged from our analysis of the children's comments written onto their questionnaires and from a study of their essays and an analysis of the teachers' reports.

Primary age children

Most *primary age children* appear to have some restrictions exercised upon their viewing of both television and video. These restrictions seem to be mainly in terms of the times of programmes, particularly on school days. The majority of parents also exercise some restrictions on the type of film their children see. A 9-year-old boy wrote 'I like horrors because they're scary and spooky, but I am not allowed to watch very very scary films.' The juniors list many ways in which they get round the restrictions exercised by parents. Typical are 'watching on another TV in the bedroom', 'sneaking downstairs and watching through a door', 'going to a friend's house and watching it there'.

The last mentioned seems to be the favourite action in watching forbidden video films. This correlates with the evidence we have received from parents that indicates that many of them are unaware of the particular videos that have been seen by their children.

Secondary age children

Among *secondary age children* there are some restrictions on most of them in the lower age groups but few, if any, upon children in the upper age groups. An 11-year-old girl who had seen the 'video nasties' said, 'My Dad doesn't like me to watch films which have too much swearing. I don't have bad dreams, but my sister does. And my sister is not allowed to watch horrors, "video nasties", or films which have swearing in.'

A 12-year-old girl stated, 'I am not allowed to watch dirty films or late films.' This girl, however, had seen no less than seven videos on the DPP's list although she had no VCR in her home. She stated that she had seen them all at a friend's house. An 11-year-old girl who said her parents placed no restrictions on her viewing listed a total of 31 videos she had seen. Seven of these were on the DPP's list and five were rated '18' adult films. Her most remembered film sequence was from *Halloween* 'where the boy chops his Mum up'. She added '*Halloween* stayed in my mind for a week.'

Children's Reaction

The teachers' reports of class discussions, individual interviews with children plus the evidence from their written comments all indicate that many children do suffer some kind of adverse reaction following the watching of violent or horrific video films. Their essays also give similar evidence. It would appear that most normal children suffer some kind of disturbance to their thought pattern or sleep pattern following the watching of particularly explicit and horrific violence. Bad dreams or nightmares are the most common reaction. It is not uncommon, however, for children to say that the most vivid sequences either in picture form or dialogue remain with them in the conscious mind through the day as well as disturbing their sleep pattern at night. This effect is usually only short-term and in the majority of cases lasts only about one week.

There are, however, other children perhaps of a more nervous disposition, where the effects take a different form and are more lasting. These children become afraid of the dark, or of being left alone. They display a variety of other symptoms of personal insecurity that affect their relationships with other children and inevitably have an effect upon their academic performance at school as well as upon their social relationships.

There were many examples given by the children of bad dreams and of the short-term effects of vivid scenes of violence. But there were many more examples given by the children of more lasting effects such as the 12-year-old girl who said, 'I am scared that there is someone behind the wardrobe who is going to jump out and stab me.' A junior age boy described how he regularly awoke in the night with nightmares and said that he sits up in bed and bangs his head until the pictures go away. He demonstrated this to the teacher by giving heavy blows to the side of his head. Quite a number of children confessed that they were too frightened to get out of bed at night to go to the bathroom in the dark.

Even secondary age children confessed to having nightmares although most also claimed that horror videos had no lasting effect upon them. They enjoyed the experience of being frightened and certainly for the boys it had become a test of manliness that they could both sit through the most violent films and suffer no harmful after-effects.

The reports indicate that girls in the upper age groups are more ready to confess to having been disturbed by horror films. In one class of 24 14-year-olds there was only one child who claimed not to have been disturbed. One girl said that she couldn't get out of her mind the scene in *The Evil Dead* where 'the woman's head is chopped off with the spade'. Many of the older children said that the disturbing effect was short-term and that they suffered no lasting ill effects, although their younger brothers and sisters were often disturbed by watching videos.

The following is a selection from children's written comments sent to us from one school.

I have Seen about 15 (B)
I watched the living Dead and I wanted
to watch it because I thought it
would be exciting But After Seeing
Some horrific Sceans I actually thought.
Scared So At The end of the silt film, I
was Feeling A bit Sick. my small Brother
walked into The room and Saw a
horrific Scean which made him have
Night-MARES.

I saw evil dead, I feel sick after.
Most films are good if they
have a good story to them. But
some can be really frightening.
I don't really think they should theses.

Because teenagers get
a bit funny. And might try things
Like rapeing girls. It might be
fun for them, but it is not
fun for us.

Evil dead = was a very frightening film,
after that film I was frightened to go
into the dark. I think that this film
should be watched by adults only.

Teachers' Comments

It is not only middle school and upper age children who watch pornography.
We have had a number of examples quoted where parents of quite young
children have allowed their infants to watch explicit sex scenes.

One teacher said that a little girl in her class had come to her and said, 'My
Mummy let me watch a nasty film last night and now I know all about sex!'
The teacher replied, 'What do you know about sex?' 'Sex' said the child, 'is
when a big man knocks you down onto the floor and gets on top of you and
you scream and you scream and you scream because it hurts.' The little girl
was only 4-years-old and the teacher was so shocked she spoke to the mother
about it, who replied, 'Well, she's got to find out about life some time hasn't
she!'

It would appear from the rape scene described by this child that this was
her introduction to human sexual activity. It is a matter of conjecture what
effect this will have upon her relationships with members of the opposite sex
later in life.

Many teachers commented upon the fact that children are emotionally
immature and cannot handle the kind of explicit sex and violence that is
portrayed so realistically in many video films. We can see the immediate or
short-term effect upon these children but there is no way of knowing what
long-term effect the exposure to this kind of material may have either upon
the formation of their moral values or their social relationships. There are
many variables that affect the child's reactions, even for normal children,
that is for those who have no apparent psychiatric problems. The degree of
security they experience from home and family as well as the strength and
even the happiness of the parents' marriage is a major variable in coping with
emotional experiences.

The following is a selection of extracts from teachers' reports all dealing
with children in the primary, that is infant and junior, age groups.

I am most concerned that these things are in a child's memory as children learn so much at this age, which is impressionable and can influence them for life. I sincerely doubt whether a child having seen a film four times will ever forget the details and I am concerned about the desire there seems to be in at least one of these children to see more . . . I refer to such films as *Carrie* and *Rosemary's Baby* which one child has seen four times on video. Children aged five and six have often seen one film a few times and can describe in detail scenes which I consider horrific.

There is good evidence to suggest that violence starts in the mind. If we fill children's minds with the imagery of violence and brutality, we may expect to see it re-emerge in verbal and physical forms, as well as in their free play, art work, creative writing and drama through which the pupils express the nature of their inner resources. This is underlined by the following extracts from teachers' reports.

Drawings often include reference to the sort of tortures and sexual violence seen in 'nasties'.

Frequently art work reflects monsters or people with knives stuck into them while blood is realistically dripping from inflicted wounds. A number of children favour subjects which incorporate scenes of horror or other violent actions. Many have a highly developed sense of the macabre.

Horror stories are very popular topics in free writing. One sees evidence of it in 'jest', as though laughing about it in their writing is a way of getting it out of their system.

In art work, illustrations of a violent nature have occasionally been noted – figures being stabbed, split open, etc. Occasionally a minority of children have written stories about characters who are beaten to death and mutilated. Subjects treated in a spirit of innocent amusement.

In free drawing, very bloodthirsty things that I would never have thought of were depicted. When asked about them the children replied that they had seen it on 'such a video'. One child wrote about being raped by a madman, another about bottles 'being shoved up inside people'.

Teachers are concerned about the swearing and the abusive and often filthy language which is now to be heard in school, the 'threats made in vicious terminology', the 'noticeable aggression and violence both in behaviour and language'. For example one teacher wrote, 'An 11-year-old boy used to tell stories using obscene language to other children. Once I heard him shout, "I'll rape you" to a 10-year-old girl.' The language children use is an indicator of what is filling their minds.

Many educationalists agree that a central task of children in adolescence is the formation of a potentially worthwhile and satisfying self-image which will be the foundation of a healthy personality. Children of school age look to their parents, teachers and peer group as well as to characters from story and screen for their models. Parents who allow their children to watch 'video nasties' are offering them criminals and psychopaths with whom to identify and who may become their patterns and influence the formation of their social values.

One teacher wrote:

> I used to be of the opinion that censorship of home videos was not really necessary as responsible adults could then watch what they wanted, and of course, they wouldn't let children watch unsuitable material. However, recently after discovering how many 7- to 8-year-olds in my class have seen very violent videos (eg *Cannibal Holocaust*, *Driller Killer*, etc.) I feel inclined to change my views on censorship.

Another expressed his fears for the future:

> One feels the tendencies towards disturbance will grow. Having watched the very popular Michael Jackson *Thriller* myself, I was sickened. It is a tragic comment on our society that millions of pounds are spent in 'entertaining people with fear'. One wonders where it will lead – and what will happen next.

> Parents are blissfully unaware of the dangers of this sort of material. Some friends of mine have recently acquired a video. Their 2/3-year-old child is subjected to all the 'video nasties'. He may watch, he may just lie dozing. The parents seem unaware that all this sort of material is 'seeping in' and influencing the child. It never ceases to amaze me, also, how educated people, including teachers, under-estimate the *power of the media* in this respect. One only has to stop and think about why TV advertising takes place at all to *prove* that it is a strong influence on people's behaviour.

Teachers are aware that other factors, such as broken homes, have a bearing on the disturbed behaviour they have reported. School is a microcosm of society, and it is generally recognised that the level of violence in society has risen. We may therefore expect this to be reflected in the behaviour of children in school. The social phenomena of violence are highly complex, especially in the area of analysing root causes. There are many variables and this presents difficulty in their isolation. Undoubtedly the media representation of violence is a major variable and the vivid portrayal of violence on video film is a powerful element. We must not, however, make the mistake of ignoring the pernicious impact of violent video films simply because there are other influences.

Behavioural Changes

Over the past few years teachers have noted some significant changes in children's behaviour. There has been an increase in behaviour suggesting emotional disturbance, withdrawal, nervousness, aggression, abusive language and a rapid resort to violence. Boys and girls have always quarrelled and fought, defied their parents and teachers, and been destructive. Teachers well know this: but the changes they comment on are more fundamental. A difference has been noted in their relationships with one another, **in their rejection of fair play, in an impulse towards cruelty and towards the macabre**.

These reports suggest that **we are beginning to create a generation of children with a different set of values from previous ones**. Their behaviour displays **less personal restraint and an increased level of violence and aggressive reaction to situations**. This is most obvious in the playground, where children feel free from restraint and make their own rules.

Violence and Aggression

The link between violent and aggressive behaviour and watching scenes of violence on video films is not easy to establish and impossible to prove without conducting controlled experiments which would be monitored. Nevertheless the evidence that such a link does exist and that the constant exposure to scenes of violence, dulls sensitivity, shapes values and influences behaviour is too great to be ignored. Commenting on this the head master of a London comprehensive school reported that a boy who had committed a number of vicious attacks upon other children admitted his addiction to 'video nasties'. He had seen at least 29 of the 51 films on the DPP's list. The headmaster sent us an extract from an essay written by this boy which we reproduce below.

The best video I liked was I spit on your grave because four men rapped a lady and she got her back by killing very badly. I think watching bloody films is that it's a new experience. People can be affected by this and even go out and do these kind of things. People have never witnessed bad killings in real life so therefore they find exciting watching something never have seen before.

The headmaster continued:

I questioned at the time whether the violent scenes he had witnessed had influenced his violent assault on a girl earlier in the term. He had been severely disciplined over this and I had hoped that he had learned his lesson.

Earlier this month, the same pupil was officially suspended by the School Governors following his attack on another boy who sustained a broken nose, bruises, abrasions and bite marks. This can be no mere coincidence. A child brought up on violence is bound to produce violence. I have no doubt in my own mind that unless something is done to curb the extreme violence portrayed in videos, films and on the television, in the coming years we will see increasing violence in society. The moral welfare of children is quite clearly at stake!

There is a general consensus of opinion among teachers from all over the country, in primary and secondary schools alike that violence and violent language are on the increase. One Head Teacher commented that in the past he would often find a ring of boys watching a fight between two of their number. Nowadays the ring of boys would all be surrounding one boy, and he would be lying on the ground trying to protect himself while they all 'put the boot in'. He said, 'Today there is no such thing as a fair fight. What we see among children is just naked aggression.'

Typical anecdotes are:

We have had children fighting, knocking one to the ground, then kicking him repeatedly in the stomach. They kick, punch and fight if provoked even slightly. The first reaction is to hurt.

Some older girls held a boy down and kicked him repeatedly in the stomach. The boy vomited and had to be sent home.

It has become most noticeable that boys' playground games have become most aggressive in recent times. There is an observable increase in intensity and passion as revealed by physical abuse; and the willingness to 'put the boot in' has changed the way in which boys settle their differences. Playground fights are not new, nor is the encouragement to 'have a go' from by-standers; but the tendency to kick someone on the ground is new and worrying.

Violent Games

Some teachers mentioned the dangers of new techniques of fighting, eg Kung Fu, and made direct connections with the screen: 'They often emulate violence they have seen on films in their play', 'I have seen children react in the manner of some recently seen hero of violence.' The influence of the screen is 'shown in games of Kung Fu where kicking others seems to be the main characteristic', 'I've found children who watch them tend to be more aggressive' and 'Some may re-enact scenes from the film or play games which culminate in a brutal "murder".'

One headmaster reported that he had had to ban a new game that the boys had developed in recent months called 'King Ball'. He said that towards the end of break time the boys would begin throwing a ball around the playground from one boy to another. When the bell sounded the luckless boy who was left holding the ball would be set upon by all the boys in the playground on their way into school. As each one passed they would aim a blow at him, hitting, punching or kicking. The head reported some quite serious injuries among boys resulting from this, including broken bones, and had had to ban the game.

A headmaster of a primary school reported that in the autumn of 1984 at the height of the miners' strike when scenes of picket line violence were continually being shown upon television news he had been startled to see similar scenes being re-enacted at his own school. During the mid-morning break he was in his study and happened to look out of the window and see the entire playground clear with one half of the children at on end and the other half at the other end. On a given signal the two companies began to charge towards the middle of the playground with a crunch encounter resulting in the whole school fighting. He rushed out into the playground to break them up, grabbed one boy out of the mêlée and asked what on earth they were doing. The child replied, 'It's alright, sir. We're playing police and miners!' If evidence were required to support the contention that children do copy the things that they see on the small screen this would be a classic.

At a conference of head teachers in a London borough there was unanimous agreement that over the past ten years there has been a noticeable increase in violent behaviour among children. Not a single head teacher disagreed with this view. There was general agreement that in their professional experience they had witnessed a noticeable increase in aggressive behaviour both in the playground and in the classroom. This aggression was to be seen in interpersonal relationships both at a peer group level among the children and between children and members of the teaching staff.

Attacks upon Teachers

There is evidence that the number of pupil attacks upon teachers has increased sharply in recent years. There have been instances of members of staff being viciously abused and attacked. One teacher wrote, 'The long dinner-time is a nightmare for all who have to supervise it.'

Little publicity is given to these attacks unless they involve legal proceedings and Local Authorities are reluctant to discuss them or to reveal figures.

Directors of Education have no wish for the schools in their area to gain an unsavoury reputation among teachers that could affect their recruitment of teaching staff.

This is a situation that is causing considerable concern to the teachers unions and associations. Mr Tom McKee, Regional Organiser in Northern Ireland of the National Association of Schoolmasters and Union of Women Teachers, reported in January 1985 that his union receives up to a hundred enquiries a year from members wishing to retire early as a direct result of stress. He spoke of physical assaults and intimidation by pupils that in his view were more the result of viewing horrific scenes of violence on video films than a consequence of the troubles in Ulster.

The NAS/UWT is presently conducting a survey in order to ascertain the extent of pupils' violence towards teachers, and they are already aware that there has been an increase in both numbers and severity of attacks upon their members.

The following letter received from the Professional Association of Teachers graphically describes the serious situation in which the teaching profession is now placed. Their General Secretary, Mr Peter Dawson, gave permission for it to be reproduced in the Report of this Enquiry.

The following gives brief details about the signatories: of the letter

Ian Mitchell Lambert Headmaster of Howbury Grange School in the London Borough of Bexley; former National Chairman of our Association; currently Chairman of our Educational Services Committee.

Noel Henderson Deputy Head of the Lawrence Jackson School in Guisborough, Cleveland; former National Chairman of our Association; currently a Vice President of our Association.

Mrs Jean Davies An ordinary classroom teacher at Howbury Grange School in the London Borough of Bexley; former National Chairman of our Association; currently a member of our elected governing Council.

Peter Dawson General Secretary of our Association; previously a practising schoolmaster for over twenty years; headmaster of Eltham Green School in the Inner London Education Authority 1970 to 1980.

Julian Bell Head of year and teacher of modern languages at Hamilton School in Leicester; current National Chairman of our Association.

Keiran Salter Classroom teacher at St Mary and St Giles C of E Middle School at Milton Keynes; the leading figure among our younger members.

THE BEHAVIOUR OF YOUNG PEOPLE IN SCHOOLS

There has been a noticeable increase in violence among children and young people in schools in recent years. They are more likely to resort to acts of physical aggression than was once the case; when they do so, the degree of violence they go in for tends to be greater than it used to be.

The days when two boys exchanged a few blows with their fists to sort out their differences are over. Today, anything goes. Fists, boots, blunt instruments and even knives are the order of the day.

Since we live at a time when authority in all its forms is under challenge, it follows that a teacher who attempts to break up a fight places himself or herself very much more at risk than in days gone by. With good reason, some teachers decline to get involved and prefer to look the other way. This, of course, does nothing to reduce the incidence of violence among young people.

It perhaps needs to be added that the greatest increase of all has been in what might be called verbal violence. The things young people will say today to their teachers would have been unthinkable twenty years ago. One of the greatest risks any young woman entering a teaching career faces at this time is that of being reduced to a state of tearful helplessness in face of a stream of foul abuse from a disgruntled pupil.

Sadly, the stage has been reached in the educational system where violence and objectionable behaviour on the part of children is now regarded as being so perfectly normal that nothing very much need or can be done about it.

Summary

There is overwhelming evidence that vast numbers of school children of all ages have seen, and continue to see, video films containing scenes of explicit sadistic cruelty. These violent videos appeal to the basest instincts in human nature and arouse sadistic feelings by dwelling in great detail on the infliction of pain, presenting it as pleasurable. There is a very real danger that exposure to such scenes of cruelty may dull the viewers' sensitivity to pain and distress and encourage the growth of perversion.

There are progressive stages in such a process of development.

1 First, the subject becomes desensitised by cruelty, and therefore unmoved by it.

2 Secondly, he experiences actual enjoyment of such scenes.

3 Thirdly, he moves from enjoying it to requiring ever increasing degrees of intensity in order to reach the same high pitch of enjoyment. *Thus the appetite for violence actually increases by being fed.*

In their thorough research into the effects of television as a moral teacher, Liebert and Poulos (1976) state:

> At the simplest level one implication of the research is clear: television is a moral teacher and a powerful one. Contemporary television entertainment is saturated with violence and related antisocial behaviour and lessons which have a clear, and by most standards, adverse effect on young viewers' development and behaviour.

They also cite evidence that an equally important outcome (of exposure to violence on the screen) is that 'children's sensitivities may be blunted to aggressive and violent actions performed by others'.

These conclusions refer to violence on television. They could equally well refer to video films in that both are visual means of communication, but the fact is that the video films of this kind that we are considering are far more potent than anything to be seen on television. They show scenes that are so depraved that they would never be passed for general viewing. More significantly, it is possible to stop a video film and run a replay of some enjoyable sequence. Children themselves have said that one of the advantages of the video is that they can play their gory and sadistic choices over and over again, printing them indelibly on the mind.

As an argument against the control of 'video nasties' it has been said that violence has always been present in the child's world of imagination – particularly in their literature. This is, of course, true; and it is also true that it would not be desirable to exclude all violence from children's stories. Their reading and viewing should portray a real world in which there is a place for beauty and ugliness; where they can find the values by which we live, usually described in the lovely words of our language as truth, justice, loyalty and faith, but where these may be seen to operate even in the face of oppression, cruelty and criminal activity. The crucial factor is how the author presents his material and directs the reader's responses.

A few years ago the violent element in nursery rhymes came under discussion. People were concerned that at such a tender age children should be introduced to the 'shocking' verses of Three Blind Mice:

They all ran after the farmer's wife,
Who cut off their tails with a carving knife,

or the 'religious bigotry' expressed in the lines:

There I met an old man
Who wouldn't say his prayers,
So I took him by the left leg
and threw him down the stairs!

One can understand this anxiety, but it overlooks the context in which the words are customarily heard, maybe on the lap of an understanding adult or in a secure nursery circle; the remote and unrealistic picture they create, and the fact that they are presented in a style which suggests that they are not meant to be believed. The stylised treatment keeps the experience at a distance and makes an acceptable vehicle for a child's fantasies.

Fairy tales and historical novels are similarly distanced. Violence on the screen, however, is a different matter. The sense of immediacy that it excites and the fact that the settings are usually close to the child's own experience render it particularly potent. A child is more likely to accept as normal scenes and actions which appear to be part of his familiar contemporary environment. Moreover, the aim of violent videos in dwelling at length on gruesome details, is patently that of exciting sadistic feelings, representing the infliction of pain as a source of pleasure.

As an educationalist I concur with David Hartshorn's view that children are well able to cope with an energetic imagination, but I am not convinced that when very strong visual and auditory images accompany such imaginings, children are equally able to cope with the confusion in their minds.

The fear of many teachers is that children will become able to tolerate scenes of ever-increasing sadism, indeed that they will seek for further horrors in order to stimulate the same level of titillation. Millions of pounds would not be spent on screen advertising unless its power to influence the mind was proven. It needs only common sense, even without supporting statistics, to see that children will carry these violent images from the world of fantasy into their real world of playground, street and home.

Finally, it needs to be recognised that a major part of a child's development and maturation is that of internalising a value system that will influence behaviour throughout life. The injection of horrific and vivid scenes of violence into that developmental process is likely to confuse the child's developing perception of morality. At a time when teachers are helping children to acquire a moral definition for life, which they instinctively seek, these violent videos run counter to their efforts, undercutting the principles and values on which the life of school and society are based. They do not show the final triumph of good, nor the moral beauty of goodness, neither do they satisfy the innate sense of justice that all children have. The end result can only be the infliction of permanent damage to children at the most susceptible and vulnerable period in their lives.

References

HARTSHORN, D. (1983) 'Children and Video Films at Home' *Educational Studies*, Vol. 9, No. 3.
LIEBERT and POULOS (1976) 'Television as a Moral Teacher' in LICHONA, T (ed) *Moral Development and Behaviour: theory, research and social issues*. New York: Holt, Rinehart and Winston.

10 Conclusion

Clifford Hill

Social Background

1 New Social Phenomenon

The social phenomenon of the use of violence for entertainment is not new. It is almost as old as mankind. Each age has had its own particular forms of violent entertainment, from the contests of gladiators or the jousting of knights, to bear-baiting and bull-fighting. What is fundamentally different in the use of violence as a means of entertainment in our present era is the media of presentation.

Modern film technology, plus the mass media of distribution through television and video, has the capability of transforming fantasy and fiction into the everyday world of reality in a powerful and often confusing manner for vast numbers of people in many nations and of all ages.

The so-called 'video nasty' is a new phenomenon not simply due to its deliberate exploitation of cruelty and sado-masochism but through its ability to transfer such scenes into the everyday settings of familiar life patterns, such as city backstreets and the home. Television and video are, moreover, powerful means of transmitting ideas. They contrast sharply to the written word. Reading requires effort. Everything is left to the imagination and the page merely triggers ideas which have to be generated from within. The video film works the other way round. The images are already provided pre-packaged, pre-edited, pre-conceived, pre-run and pre-digested. Because it requires no effort on the part of the recipient, it may be received uncritically and its values internalised without conscious effort.

2 In The Home

The video cassette recorder is rapidly becoming a major source of home entertainment. Britain has the highest density of VCRs per head of the population of any nation in the world. With the current rate of expansion, it is probable that the VCR could become as common in British homes as is the television. The opening up of this new market has generated a new outlet for films, thousands of which have already been transferred to videotape and thus made available for home viewing. It has also opened the way for video films to be produced especially for the home viewing market.

While it is comparatively simple to control what films are shown in places of public exhibition, it is very much more difficult to control what is shown in millions of individual homes. It is also incontravertible that what is available in the home will be available to children. Even with the most careful parents, as our evidence shows, young children do see adult rated video films especially where there are older teenage children within the family. It is thus very difficult to protect children from exposure to unsuitable video films that are freely available for home viewing.

3 Fact and Fantasy

The point has been made by both consultant psychiatrists and educationalists in this study that the present era of violent video films cannot be compared with the violence depicted in children's stories of previous generations. Folk stories and fiction for both children and adults of former eras usually had 'a happy ending'. The perpetrator of violence was never the hero and it was an unwritten law that good would inevitably triumph over evil in the end.

The video film of today has no such underlying assumptions. In many cases cruelty and extreme acts of violence against the human body are deliberately exploited in order to shock, excite and thrill. This is sometimes done in a pseudo-documentary style but with the same objective. Thus the world of fiction and folklore which traditionally was closely linked with the transmission of the cultural values of that society has, with the advent of the video film, been divorced from any concept of morality or desire to communicate a cultural norm. Thus the way has been opened for the commercial exploitation of a powerful medium of communication by those whose primary objective is commercial gain.

4 New Concept

Another new concept of the video film that has been freely exploited by the producers of the most explicit scenes of violence on video film has been a fundamental shift in the standpoint from which violence is viewed. As with traditional fiction through folklore and through the written pages of books, so too an earlier generation of films were made to depict violence from the standpoint of an on-looker or from that of the victim of aggression. The reader or viewer was then able to experience revulsion from the act of violence, anger with the aggressor and compassion for the victim.

The modern portrayal of violence is often depicted from the standpoint of the aggressor rather than the victim of aggression, so that the viewer is able to participate in the act of aggression and savour the horror of the victim and often mentally disturbed emotions of sado-masochists and psychopathic killers. The dangers of marketing such material to the general public and especially of exposing young immature children to such scenes is regarded by the consultant psychiatrists in this Enquiry to be considerable. They are particularly concerned about the effects upon those with a tendency towards aggression.

5 Social Change

The full significance of the advent of the VCR, and in particular of the development of the video film containing scenes of extreme violence, can only be appreciated within the context of a sociological analysis of current processes of change. Although aggression and violence have been character-istics of human behaviour since the dawn of mankind, it is demonstrable that overt levels of violence are increasing both at an international level through the application of science and technology to the weapons of mass destruction and at a societal level through the complex interaction of forces of change within the growth pattern and development of urban industrial societies.

Sociologists recognise five major institutions, or areas of organised social life. These are: (1) The family; (2) The economy; (3) Education; (4) Law and Government; (5) Religion and Morality (Belief Systems and Values). In studying these institutions, particularly in structural functional terms, within the context of the processes of change that govern and modify them, sociologists recognise a fundamental theoretical principle; namely, that where change occurs within one major social institution some modification occurs in all the others. A radical change in one social institution affects all the other areas of social life.

One simple illustration of this principle may be seen in the industrial revolution which produced a fundamental change in the economy through a change in the means of production. This affected the family by drawing people away from simple village life in rural communities and agrarian pursuits to urban complexes and industrial occupations. Education had to be formalised and thus became centred outside the family. Changes in law and law enforcement were required to meet the new forms of social interaction; and belief systems and values were inevitably changed through the bringing together of people from different cultures and the development of wider means of communication. One could similarly illustrate concomitant changes that occur in other areas of social life where changes are generated within any of the major social institutions.

Throughout the Western world today, and indeed in many areas of the developing world, a new and unique social phenomenon has been occurring throughout recent decades that is producing a highly complex and volatile social situation extremely difficult to analyse. It is this – each of our major institutions is generating rapid, radical and fundamental change at the same time. Thus each is producing change factors that modify the other social institutions at the very same time as change is being generated from within those institutions. The consequence is a period of rapid and radical change, hitherto unknown to the sociologist, and probably unique in human history.

A high level of change creates a very volatile social situation with considerable structural strains within all parts of the social system. In other words, it means that society itself becomes unstable. In simple terms, society, as the aggregate of human beings, bears many of the characteristics of the individual personality. There is a limit to the amount of fundamental changes that each individual can experience and absorb within a given period of time without experiencing instability and insecurity, resulting in uncharacteristic behaviour or even breakdown. For example, if a person experiences marriage breakdown, loss of family, loss of job and possibly loss of home all in a very short space of time, it may very likely result in some form of breakdown. The capacity to absorb change will, of course, vary from individual to individual. This is also true for societies but the fact remains that each society or national group does have a limit to its capacity to absorb radical change in all its significant areas of social organisation without experiencing the shaking of its foundations through the challenge to established norms that normally provide a large measure of social stability.

In a situation of rapid and radical social change such as we have today, the established social values underlying the norms that form the foundational bedrock upon which the whole social system rests are being challenged by a multitude of complex interacting forces which are evidenced in the phenomenology of behaviour at both an individual and a societal level. The young are particularly susceptible to the effects of the instability surrounding foundational social values.

The process of socialisation through which the culture of a society is transmitted from one generation to another, which includes both the formal educational process and the transmission of ideas, values and behavioural norms, is at its peak during childhood and adolescence. In order for the maturation process to develop through to normal healthy stable adult lives, the ideal situation is that the values transmitted during childhood and adolescence should have some quality of constancy.

In the highly volatile and fluid social situation that pertains in many societies today even foundational social values are being challenged and the pre-packaged norms underlying or implied by the scenes of violence portrayed in many video films are a powerful means of transmitting new social values at a time when the old values are no longer holding firm and society is open to internalise new cultural norms. The VCR thus needs to be seen in its full sociological significance at such a period in history when new norms may be easily transmitted and may swiftly become foundational values in a society.

Research Results

1 Exposure of children

The figures derived from the National Viewers' Survey conducted as part of this Enquiry revealed that large numbers of schoolchildren of all ages have been and are being exposed to films primarily intended for an adult market. The sample of families visited by Officers of the NSPCC together with data derived from other sources in the Enquiry indicates that many children of pre-school age are also being exposed to video films of this nature. The conclusion is that whatever is available for home viewing will be seen by children of all ages.

The current trend among some film makers of producing video films especially for the home market, that they know would not obtain certification for public exhibition, has resulted in the availability of films containing scenes of extreme violence that even the most liberal-minded producers and distributors did not intend to be seen by children. The British Videogram Association and other spokesmen representing the distributors have constantly dissociated themselves from any intention to expose children to the so-called 'video nasties' or other specifically adult material. But the fact is that a great many school children have actually seen a video film containing scenes of extreme violence. This is an undeniable conclusion from this Enquiry.

The sceptics are, of course, perfectly entitled to question the figures produced by our research and we freely acknowledge the difficulties of obtaining accurate information on this subject. Children are notoriously unreliable respondents. But so are adults! It is a recognised fact of any piece of social investigation that the use of self-completed questionnaires will produce unreliable statistical information unless there are a variety of built-in safeguards. Such techniques were faithfully used in our research and in presenting our findings to the public we believe ourselves to be social scientists of integrity who have taken all reasonable care to produce reliable figures. We would nevertheless like to make this point, that even if we are mistaken and our statistics are wildly inaccurate (although we most certainly do not believe them to be inaccurate) but if they were 10% or even 15% inaccurate – which is far beyond the normal limits of tolerance in modern social investigation – we would still have a situation in Britain in which approximately one-third of all British school children have been exposed to video films containing such scenes of extreme violence that they have been found to be legally obscene in a Court of law in the UK.

2 Effects upon Children

The evidence produced in this Enquiry strongly suggests that children are adversely affected by their exposure to scenes of violence on video film. Normal, healthy children are affected in the short-term and may suffer disturbed sleep or other forms of anxiety reaction. As regards the long-term effects, nothing can yet be said with certainty as the VCR is a new social phenomenon. The indications suggest that the short-term harmful effects do not last long in normal, healthy children especially where there is wise parental support and a secure family and home environment. Where such basic security is lacking, the harmful effects may last longer and may do permanent damage.

3 Attraction to Violence

The evidence suggests that those who have a tendency towards violence or aggressive behaviour are attracted to the viewing of violent video films. The stronger the propensity towards aggression, the stronger the attraction to viewing scenes of violence.

The evidence suggests that the viewing of scenes of extreme violence has an obsessive characteristic that may be habit forming in a manner that demands increasing stimulation through more extreme forms of violence. This is probably the result of the 'desensitisation' process whereby normal healthy people, whose first reaction to violence is one of repugnance gradually become desensitised to it through continual exposure.

4 Link with Behaviour

The evidence strongly suggests a causal link between the viewing of violence and violent behaviour. It is recognised that this is a complex issue and that it is virtually impossible to eliminate all other variables, and just isolate only the experimental variable of viewing scenes of violence, which would provide positive proof. However, the link has occurred in the evidence of so many professional people at work among children that the evidence must be considered conclusive.

The copying of behaviour seen on television and film is a well-known phenomenon. The behaviour of children emerging from a cinema reveals what kind of film they have been seeing. Teachers regularly say that they know what was on television the previous night by what games the children play the next morning. The copying of scenes viewed on video film is therefore a well-known and well established phenomenon. The evidence in this Enquiry suggests a causal link between the viewing of scenes of extreme violence and actual violent behaviour in some children and young people.

5 Catharsis Theory

The evidence from this Enquiry appears conclusively to explode the carth-
arsis theory. There was a 75% response rate of consultant psychiatrists in the
survey carried out through the Royal College of Psychiatry. Not one
psychiatrist expressed the opinion that the viewing of scenes of extreme
violence may enable a person to live out a horrific experience in fantasy or
imagination and thus prevent them from carrying out such an act in reality.
Of those psychiatrists who had found some evidence of a violent video film
being influential in a patient's emotional state or behaviour, 77% believed
that the viewing of violent videos could be harmful or disturbing and 79% of
those who believed that viewing violent videos could be harmful had found
an association between their patient's symptoms and the viewing of violent
video films. The paediatricians also produced similar results.

6 Parents' Attitudes

The evidence strongly suggests that the attitudes of the parents is a major
determinant affecting the child's viewing patterns. Where parents' attitudes
are strongly protective, comparatively few of their children have been
exposed to violent video films. In contrast, where the parents' attitudes are
broadly tolerant and children are left free to watch whatever they wish,
proportionately more of their children have watched violent video films.

This pattern is remarkably demonstrated by the NSPCC's sample. In
those families where the parents themselves watch video films portraying
scenes of extreme violence, a very high proportion of the children have been
exposed to this type of film, whereas in families where the parents do not
watch these films the proportion of children who have seen violent video
films drops dramatically.

The evidence we have examined suggests that in some families where there
is a history of violent behaviour, including child abuse, there is an attraction
to viewing violent video films. If our evidence concerning a link between
exposure to violence and violent behaviour is correct then we may well be
indicating here one of the major sources of the growth of a syndrome of
violence as a social phenomenon. Clearly this is an area that warrants further
investigation.

7 Further Research

Our Enquiry results indicate a number of areas requiring further research. In
view of the present public concern over the level of violence in society we
would advocate a major research programme into the individual and social
sources of violence. We urgently need to increase both our knowledge and
understanding of these complex issues.

Other Considerations

1 Williams Report

The Report of the Committee on Obscenity and Film Censorship presented to Parliament in 1979 has played a significant part in forming a definitive background to Home Office thinking in recent years. Although the Report dealt primarily with explicit sexual material, it also made reference to films with a violent content – especially those with the mixture of violence and sexual behaviour.

The Williams Committee received evidence from expert witnesses both for and against the link between media violence and violence in society. They concluded: 'we consider the only objective verdict must be one of "not proven"'. The committee saw no evidence of a 'causal link' between pornography and violent sexual crime and took the view that its effects were more frequently 'beneficial rather than harmful'. The Committee gave credence to the cathartic effect of such material and the possibility of such films 'assuaging the violent feelings' of people who might otherwise commit violent sexual crimes.

In terms of the 'psychological desensitisation to violence' dealt with in section 6.75, the Committee took the view that the evidence did not support such a theory 'and that there were no indications that a person's ability to feel pity and willingness to help the victim of an act of aggression was lessened by watching representations of similar acts of violence'.

The evidence of this Enquiry is directly opposed to the conclusion reached by the Williams Committee. The cathartic theory is seen to be untenable and the evidence of desensitisation to scenes of violence through continual exposure is firmly established.

To conclude, therefore, as Williams does that the availability of violent material on film has little or no effect upon the levels of violence in society is clearly mistaken.

2 Legislation

The evidence of this Enquiry is that very large numbers of children have been exposed, and continue to be exposed, to scenes of extreme violence on video film, viewed in the home. These are films that they would not legally be allowed to see in a place of public entertainment. Such films are normally dealt with under the Obscene Publications Act 1959. The weakness of the Act is notorious, particularly in relation to its definition of obscenity as 'the tendency to deprave and corrupt' which has been with us since 1868 and has formed the basis of common law since that time. The difficulty of interpreting this phrase is experienced not only by magistrates but is manifold when attempted by a jury.

The OPA 1959 could become a more effective legal instrument in protecting children from exposure to a wide range of adult material if the phrase 'a tendency to deprave and corrupt' were interpreted in the light of available evidence relating to those who are likely to see such films.

If the evidence of this Enquiry is accepted it will be seen that whatever is available for home viewing will be seen by children, and we believe that the case has been effectively made that exposure to scenes of violence does have a harmful effect on children. Therefore video films which are produced primarily for the home viewing market need to be treated in law in a different category from anything that is available for public exhibition. **Thus the implications are that material that is harmful to children should not be available for the home viewing market.**

The Video Recordings Act 1984 was specifically designed to deal with video films for the home viewing market. At the time of writing this Report, the Act had not come into force due to the large backlog of films that had to be certified by the Board of Film Censors. It has yet to be discovered how effective the Act may be in providing protection for children in home viewing. One apparent loophole is that of the direct order mailing enterprises where uncensored films may be sent direct to the home viewer in plain wrappers.

We believe our evidence establishes a clear case for careful censorship and stringent controls upon video films available for the home viewing market. This at least demands a review of existing law and its practice and interpretation. It may also require some additional legislation in order to deal with the new social phenomenon of the increasingly widespread use of the VCR in British homes and the demonstrable effects of the exposure of children and young people to scenes of extreme violence.

Where sexual behaviour is also linked with aggressive behaviour and coercion, the whole subject of pornography and its availability on the home viewing market also warrants careful review.

3 The Future

We recognise that the concept of censorship is repugnant to most British people. Freedom of choice, freedom of expression, and a wide range of individual and corporate freedoms have been an integral and deeply cherished part of the British heritage and national culture over many centuries. We do not lightly surrender our freedoms which have been fought for, established and maintained by our forefathers. These freedoms stem as much from our religious as our cultural heritage.

In order rightly to evaluate the significance of the present social situation that confronts us, we need to understand both the nature of the concept of freedom that is encapsulated in the British culture and also the nature of the new social phenomenon with which we are presented today.

We have noted in our evidence the new characteristics of the type of violence for entertainment that is being offered through the medium of the video film. We have also noted the evidence for its likely effects upon behaviour through the influence upon cultural values. In order to gauge the significance of this as a social process, we need to remind ourselves of the manner in which social values are transmitted.

The process of socialisation through which the norms of behaviour and the cultural values of society are transmitted from one generation to the next is the primary source of influencing the code of human conduct. The means of transmission in non-industrial societies, including pre-industrial Britain, is through the family and tribe. As an outcome of the Industrial Revolution the process of socialisation became more complex. Education became formalised, and the institutional means of the transmission of the culture thus became family, education, plus a variety of peer group influences in neighbourhood and environment.

Today the process has become even more complex as these institutions have been joined by the mass media. In fact, many sociologists would argue that the mass media is at least as powerful in the transmission of cultural values as other institutions, particularly in a day when the major social institutions of the family and education are weakening. The media is thus taking on a new significance in the socialisation of the young and the formation of social values and codes of behavioural conduct.

We therefore believe that our evidence establishes the case for the need to review fundamentally the role of the State in the control of the media especially in the area of television and video films. We need to ask some fundamental questions concerning the nature of the social and cultural values that we wish to transmit.

Do we wish to convey the values of violent aggression as the norm for achieving the objects of ego desire including the use of torture, cruelty, sado-masochism and even the dismemberment of the human body as behavioural norms?

Alternatively, do we wish to present the norms of harmonious interpersonal relationships, with marriage and stable family life as the model for child rearing, within the context of the ideals of a caring, sharing society?

It is possible that we may be seeing the consequences of the scenes of violence that have been transmitted through the media to children and young people in the violence that has exploded on football terraces and in our city streets.

It is now becoming of vital significance for the health and future stability of society that we recognise the social sources of violence. Merely to ban alcohol from football grounds and issue identity cards to possible malefactors is rather like directing a hose pipe at the edge of a forest fire while others are dropping paraffin on the centre of the blaze from the air.

There is an urgent need to tackle the social sources of violence and to recognise the complexity of these issues and that a simplistic approach will not suffice. The complexities of the social phenomena of violence in modern society need to be fully recognised in a day of high unemployment and soaring levels of relative deprivation in an acquisitive society against an environmental background of urban anomie. These are conditions that do not naturally produce a healthy stable society and to inject elements into the socialisation of children that deliberately promulgate the values of violence and the behavioural code of aggression is not simply the height of folly but an act of social suicide.

We recognise that to implement our findings in terms of legislation would require considerable political courage in the context of the high value British people place upon personal freedom especially that relating to our behaviour within the sanctuary of our own homes. We nevertheless believe that modern society is faced with a fundamental ethical choice that is new to our generation where advanced technology together with the processes of urbanisation and industrialisation have coalesced and have together been compounded by the process of secularisation in a manner that now challenges the foundations of our entire social fabric.

Perhaps the ultimate question facing us is, have the libertarians the right to exercise their freedom to the point at which they destroy the freedom of others? In considering this question we need to recognise the extent to which commercial forces and vested interests have joined hands with those who hold firm libertarian ethical views to confuse the issues.

We believe that the rate of change in modern society is sufficiently high to give urgency to the need for the recognition of the consequences of the forces that are at work in our society. It may well be that all our freedoms are being challenged to an extent unique in history. When the level of the breakdown of social order reaches a certain point a situation is created wherein left-wing revolutions occur or right-wing dictators after the pattern of Hitler may arise and pose as social saviours. They may be eagerly supported by those who see no other alternative to the chaos in society, and thus they achieve power.

We do not wish to be melodramatic, but we do desire to emphasise the serious social consequences of our findings. We are faced with a fundamental choice concerning the kind of society in which we wish to live. Today we still have the choice. Tomorrow we may not.

Appendix 1

Definition of the Term 'Video Nasty'

In this book we are not using the term 'video nasty' to refer to pornography, either soft porn or hard porn. In our Report Part I we defined the term 'video nasty' as those feature films that contain scenes of such violence and sadism involving either human beings or animals that they would not be granted a certificate by the British Board of Film Censors (BBFC) for general release for public exhibition in Britain. Such films may be liable to prosecution by the Director of Public Prosecutions under the Obscene Publications Act 1959 Section 2.

Appendix 2

Videos on the DPP's List

In the summer of 1983 when this research was designed, a list of thirty-two violent horror films ('video nasties') available on video cassette was obtained from conversations with officers of Scotland Yard's Vice Squad and officers from the Obscene Publications department of provincial forces. This list contains titles of video feature films that had been found obscene under the Obscene Publications Act 1959 or were at that time currently the subject of legal proceedings or being considered for prosecution by the Director of Public Prosecutions. We have called this list 'the DPP's list'. The list is as follows:

Absurd
The Beast in Heat
Blood Feast
Bloody Moon
Bogey Man
The Burning
Cannibal Apocalypse
Cannibal Ferox
Cannibal Holocaust
Cannibal Man
Cannibal Terror
Contamination
Death Trap
Don't go in the House
Don't go in the Woods Alone
Driller Killer
Faces of Death
House on the Edge of the Park
I Spit on Your Grave
The Last House on the Left
The Living Dead
Mardi Gras Massacre

Night of the Demon
Nightmares in a Damaged Brain
Possession
Pranks
Snuff
SS Experiment Camp
The Slayer
Zombie Creeping Flesh
Zombie Flesh-Eaters
Zombie Terror

A further list of 100 most popular video films was obtained from video traders. The list contains those video feature films which were hired the most times in the period leading up to the beginning of this research. The two lists were put together, randomised and inserted into the questionnaire that was put to the children in the National Viewers' Survey.

The children were not asked which video films they had seen or not seen, which would have biased the result. Instead they were asked to score on a three-point scale any that they had seen.

Since the summer of 1983 the list of titles on the DPP's list has increased from thirty-two to fifty-one (January 1984). The additional titles are given below:

Anthropophageous Beast
Blood Bath
The Beyond
* Dead and Buried
Delirium
Don't Go Near The Park
* The Evil Dead
* Evil Speak
Forest of Fear
House By the Cemetery
Island of Death
I Miss Your Hugs and Kisses
Killer Nun
Madhouse
Nightmare Maker
Night of the Bloody Apes
Prisoner of a Cannibal God
Shogun Assassin
The Burning
Toolbox Murders
Unhinged

By chance, three of the new titles (starred) were among the 100 most popular titles supplied by the video trade and therefore appeared on our question-naire. These were not included in the raw statistics published in our Report Part I, so that the figures in Chapter 4 do not directly relate to those published in the interim Report.

Appendix 3

Synopses of Videos

The Evil Dead
Zombie Flesh-Eaters
The Living Dead
The Bogey Man
The Burning
I Spit on Your Grave
Death Trap
Zombie Creeping Flesh
Zombie Terror
Driller Killer

Below are brief synopses of each of these ten films in the versions in which they have been seen on video. The descriptions are drawn from a variety of sources including trade descriptions in video magazines and journals, descriptions on the boxes of video cassettes, and synopses that have been presented in court as evidence by the prosecution.

The Evil Dead

This film is described on the cassette as 'the ultimate experience in gruelling terror. *Evil Dead* is a visual and aural attack on the senses which requires a strong stomach and a healthy sense of humour. Whilst holidaying in the Tennessee woodlands, five innocent teenagers unwittingly unleash the spirit of the evil dead which possesses first the trees and then the bodies of the friends themselves. The demonic monsters can only be halted in their frenzied flesh-eating rampage by the act of bodily disembodiment. Tensions mount as one by one the teenagers fall victim to the diabolical Sumerian spirit until finally, amid a tour de force display of special effects, the lone survivor solves the mystery which has unleashed the nightmarish terror.'

College friends Ash, Cheryl, Linda, Scott and Shelley drive to the wooded mountains of Tennessee to spend a weekend in an isolated cabin where an unseen demon lurks in the woods. In the cabin's cellar, the youngsters discover an ancient book bound in human skin and a tape-recording left by an archaeologist who had used the book to summon a pack of Sumerian demons who possessed his wife and could only be exorcised by dismemberment of the host. Playing the tape releases the evil forces. Venturing into the woods, Cheryl is molested by possessed vines entwining her body, ripping away her clothing and apparently raping her with a branch entering her vagina. Hysterically she persuades Ash to drive her to town but a vital bridge has been wrecked in a storm and Cheryl, now possessed, stabs her friend and is beaten into a cellar.

Shelley also comes under demonic influence and attacks Ash and Scott with an axe. They use the axe to chop her to pieces and a hand is eaten. They bury the apparently still-living remains. Linda then becomes possessed and attacks the two men, inflicting stab wounds and tearing flesh from one of the men's legs. Ash kills Linda in a struggle and buries her but she erupts from the grave and has to be decapitated with a spade. Scott staggers back into the cabin and dies only to be resurrected. Cheryl escapes from the cellar and is shot at close range.

Two demons repeatedly assault Ash and one has his eyes gouged out. Ash throws the book into the flames. Cheryl and Scott disintegrate, their bowels discharged, as the demons burst out of them. At dawn Ash steps out of the cabin and is overwhelmed by the unseen demon.

Zombie Flesh-Eaters

This video film is described on the cassette thus: 'When the earth spits out the dead they will return to tear the flesh of the living. In Hudson Bay a sailing boat that has a neglected appearance is drifting slowly out to sea. A coastguard boat draws up alongside and a policeman goes into the cabin. His colleagues do not see him come out again and one is about to go into the cabin when a terrifying sight appears up the hatchway – a man, covered in blood, walks towards him menacingly. Only after being hit repeatedly by bullets from a policeman's gun does he fall overboard and disappear amid the waves. This news causes a sensation and panic in the whole of America, also because the sailing boat belonged to a famous scientist who disappeared rather mysteriously in the Caribbean. The scientist's daughter, Ann, together with Peter West, a famous American journalist, set out to look for him. The two of them set sail on a schooner belonging to Brian, a young American ethnologist, and Susan, a young underwater photographer. Far out at sea Susan dives to take some photographs, but is attacked by a huge shark; however, she is saved by a zombie who unexpectedly appears out of the depths of the ocean. In the meantime, on Matul Island, in the Antilles, Professor Menard is carrying out strange experiments. What follows in the Caribbean and later in New York is terrifying – ZOMBIE FLESH-EATERS are here!!'

On Matul Island Professor Menard is carrying out experiments on the many native patients in his ramshackle hospital; his distraught wife Paola wants to leave the island. When his patients die he shoots them in the head. As the four travellers near Matul, Susan decides to dive to take photographs. Escaping from a shark, she is grasped by a zombie but manages to break free. The zombie then goes for the shark and bites lumps out of it, enabling Susan to reach the boat safely. They land and meet Menard who tells them Ann's father is dead. He then directs them to his home, not knowing that his wife has already been attacked by the zombies. The four rush away to an ancient cemetery which is disgorging corpses. Susan is killed but becomes a zombie. The other three reach the hospital and attack the zombies with rifles and Molotov cocktails; Menard is killed and Brian is bitten by Susan. He later dies and the radio brings news that New York is over-run with zombies.

Scenes of violence include a severed hand shown on a table covered with blood; a man tearing the skin from a zombie; a shark biting a zombie's hand off; a woman being attacked by a zombie and a wooden spike being shown menacing her eye. A zombie is seen with maggots on his body attacking a woman who falls to the ground covered in blood. A man shoots a zombie and strikes the zombie on the head with an axe, splitting the head open and exposing blood and other matter inside the head. The bloody body of a woman is shown. Zombie figures are seen shot several times with blood on the body. A man is shot in the head and the bloody head of a man is shown.

The Living Dead

This video film is described on the cassette as 'a horror film that will make your flesh crawl. Rejuvenating themselves on the flesh of the living, the dead are revived to walk again and torment the tormentors. A clever film with twist after twist right to the final horrific climax.'

This film shows numerous scenes of violence against the human body, both alive and dead. There are scenes of men being attacked with an axe, of disembowelling and various cannibalistic acts.

The Bogey Man

Brother and sister, Willie and Lacey, are children. Willie is tied up by his mother's brutish lover after he watches the couple making love. Young Willie is freed by his sister, Lacey, and then stabs the lover to death with the knife Lacey used to cut him free. The story then concerns the dead man's posthumous attempts at revenge resulting in numerous deaths. Scenes of violence include a man strangling a woman, a woman stabbing herself in the throat with scissors and a man stabbed through the neck with a prong.

The Burning

This is described on the cassette box as follows: 'On a moonlit evening many years ago, a group of young campers played a trick on Cropsy, the camp caretaker. The trick backfired, and Cropsy became a horribly disfigured maniac, a mutilated killer with a thirst for revenge. This is the terrifying account of Cropsy's return and the trail of blood he leaves in the dark woods.'

This film begins with the screaming Cropsy burning from head to foot and eventually falling into the lake. Five years later, horribly scarred, he is released from hospital and murders a prostitute by stabbing her in the chest. Her blood-covered body is seen to fall backwards through a window. Cropsy sets about carrying out his revenge upon a group of young people on a canoeing trip. He stabs Karen in the chest with a large pair of shears and then in a scene of explicit violence Cropsy stabs a boy in the chest, another in the throat. A boy's fingers are cut off and he is then stabbed in the eye. A girl's arm is cut off and she is stabbed in the forehead. Another young couple are murdered while participating in an explicit sex act. A young man is stabbed through the throat by garden shears and is carried by the assailant whilst held up by the shears. Another young man is slashed across the forehead by shears. Yet another attack with the shears pins a boy against a wall. In a final scene of violence with more stabbings Cropsy is eventually hit on the head with an axe and pinned to the wall and then set alight with a flame-thrower.

I Spit on Your Grave

This video film is described on the cassette as: 'A violent, shocking story of bloody revenge. Jennifer is a New York magazine writer on a vacation in an isolated countryside. While secluded in the house she has rented she meets Matthew, a semi-retarded man who delivers groceries for the local store. Seeing the reverence and desire that Matthew has for her, some of the men in the town determine to make Jennifer his first sexual experience. They kidnap her, strip her, and present her to Matthew. He retreats in fear, but Johnnie rapes her. She escapes.

'As she tries to find her way home, the men ambush her, beat her and rape her again. They leave her, and she makes her way home. But inside the house the men wait for her. When she enters, they beat her and harass her. Matthew eventually gives in to his friends' coaxing and participates in the rape. The men leave the bloody, unconscious woman on the floor of the house.

'Later they return to the house to find out if Jennifer is really dead. Seeing the men awakes an animal rage within her and she turns into a creature with no emotions and only one goal – revenge! She kills each man in a unique, elaborate manner. She makes love to Matthew and then hangs him. She seduces Johnnie in the bathtub and castrates him. The others go out to avenge their friends' murders only to confront Jennifer and come to violent and shocking ends.'

There are numerous explicit scenes of violence in this film which may be summarised as follows. Three men strip a woman against her will. One man rapes the woman whilst she is being held down by the other men. The woman is again held down by three men whilst she is raped by one man. The woman is held, kicked and beaten by the men and there is another rape. The woman is then seen in the bathtub apparently covered in blood and there follows a scene of sexual intercourse. The woman puts a rope around the man's neck and proceeds to hang him. The woman forces a man to strip at gunpoint. She castrates the man in the bath and there is a scene of a man covered in blood especially in his genital area. There is a further scene of a dead man covered in blood and another of the woman burying an axe in a man's back followed by a scene of a man covered in blood in the river. Finally the woman starts the engine of a boat when the blades are in his genital area apparently castrating him and leaving his body covered in blood in the river.

Death Trap

This video film is described on the cassette as follows: 'A sexually perverted homicidal maniac uses his run-down hotel to attract victims who will not be missed. The bodies – sometimes still alive – are thrown to a huge crocodile. *Texas Chain Saw Massacre* director Tobe Hooper gives you another orgy of blood and terror!'

The scenes of violence in this video film include a man raping a woman, a man continuously stabbing a woman with a rake and scenes of her body covered in blood. A dog is eaten by a crocodile. A man stabs another man with a scythe and he is then eaten by the crocodile. A man beats a woman around the head with his hand after having tied her up. A further scene is of a woman tied up on a bed and beaten. A man impales another man on a scythe through his neck and then throws him to the crocodile. A man pushes another man into the pond and he is then eaten by the crocodile. A man attacks a woman and pushes her through the balustrade. And finally a man is eaten by a crocodile.

Zombie Creeping Flesh and *Zombie Terror*

Although having different story lines these are similar in scenes of violence and cannibalism to those already described in *Zombie Flesh-Eaters*.

Driller Killer

Driller Killer is described on the box as follows: 'The blood runs in rivers. As the screaming drill closes on its victims you don't really believe what you are seeing, until the blood starts pouring and another tearing scream joins the drill. A steel stomach is required to watch the final scenes of mayhem.'

The scenes of violence in this video film include a skinned rabbit being hung by its rear legs, gutted and dismembered. The carcass is then mutilated and beaten. An electric drill is placed in a man's back. Blood is seen spurting out. He is also drilled in the chest and his body mutilated with the drill. The drill is placed in another man's chest and blood spurts out. Two more men are drilled in the back and in various parts of the body. A man is drilled in the head. Another man is nailed through both hands and then apparently killed with the drill. There is a scene of the mutilated body of a man and yet another similar scene. Finally a man is held and apparently drilled in the back.

Index